WALLACE STEVENS

Wallace Stevens

An approach to his poetry and thought

by ROBERT PACK

GORDIAN PRESS
NEW YORK
1968

Originally Published 1958
Reprinted 1968

Library of Congress Catalogue Card Number: 68-24044

Published by GORDIAN PRESS, by arrangement
with Rutgers, The State University

CONTENTS

WALLACE STEVENS

INTRODUCTION

For Wallace Stevens, the imagination, after its most adventurous and extravagant flights, always returned to its
natural home in the ordinary setting of Hartford, Connec-
ticut. The ordinary, Stevens believed, is always what one
makes of it, and Stevens' poetic energy was released in his
response to an ordinary world. What matters is what the
artist adds to life in living it, in bringing to it the fullness
of his response, and the inventions that this response includes. "The relation of art to life is of the first importance
especially in a skeptical age since, in the absence of a belief
in God, the mind turns to its own creations and examines
them, not alone from the aesthetic point of view, but for
what they reveal, for what they validate and invalidate,
for the support that they give." (*Opus Post.*, p. 159)

Stevens is the perfect example of the contemporary Western sophisticate. He is not obsessed with any social ideology or political movement, but assumes his heritage of freedom, the routine of living that has been handed on to him. He comes to the defense of what already is and finds the point of life in the satisfactions of life. He is more interested in continuity than in progress, for the life of the imagination does not improve, but continues embodied in the great men of each age. The richness of the mind does not become exhausted, and therefore life does not. Cosmopolitan though he is, Stevens' poetry is filled with American scenes, places and persons: the Carolinas, New England, Tallapoosa, Norfolk, Key West, Jersey City, Philadelphia, Hartford, New Haven, Bucks County; Negroes, politicians, farmers, society women, and soldiers. Stevens surveys the panorama of his thoughts, for ideas, not Americana, are his central concern. And this above all typifies the "new American intellectual," who sees himself as belonging first to the great stream of Western culture and thinks of himself only secondarily as part of a particular country, group or community. He feels as closely allied to Plato as to Jefferson, to Proust and Dostoevsky as to Mark Twain.

But there is another element in Stevens' Americanism, and that is his cosmic optimism and sense of human fraternity. Are his words not reminiscent of Whitman when he says: "Follow after, O my companion, my fellow, my self,/ Sister and solace, brother and delight." With Stevens, such words do not carry the same boisterousness and overtness as do Whitman's, but the spirit is there, the same love for mankind, the delight in energy and in life. If it has become a more intellectual energy, a love less demonstrated than philosophically held, it reflects less a fundamental change in outlook than the greater sophistication of our times. We are, one hundred years after Whitman, less exuberant, less boyish, less adventurous; we take fewer physical risks, and we think of life's danger in existential or in psychological terms.

There can be no doubt but that we are living in the apocalyptic hour. And the emotion we share, as before any catastrophe, is one of incredulity; we refuse to believe that it can happen. And perhaps we are right, perhaps our claims about the imminence of self-destruction are grandiose and vain, the irony of such a possibility too great to be true. Whatever the reason, it seems that our concern and fear of this possibility lack an ultimate seriousness and conviction. Indeed, the very helplessness we feel, or rather the helplessness to which we submit, is the inability to summon this conviction, and the paradox of this helplessness, this inability, is that it comforts us, and we turn from our apocalyptic consciousness to the little engagements of our daily lives.

In such an hour, what wisdom is most precious? Is it the prophetic voice reminding us of what we cannot bear to know; or is it the voice that says: to witness through the artist's eye, even Hamlet's tragic fall, is to be in paradise? To say that all things are potentially beautiful, for there is nothing beyond the touch of the artist, may not be the last reach in the paradox of human understanding, but at least it indicates the kind of paradise that may be lost if the prophetic voice is right. This paradise, rich with the transformation the imagination makes of ordinary experience, is what Wallace Stevens envisions and evolves, it is the treasure most accessible to our modest lives, and for many it would define the sum of human loss were it to be relinquished.

R.P.

ONE

The Comic Spirit

✲ Yet the quotidian saps philosophers
And men like Crispin like them in intent,
If not in will, to track the knaves of thought.

There is no contradiction between imagination and reality in the poetry of Wallace Stevens; he is concerned with an antinomy. As he regards the flourishing and mystery of human consciousness, he is neither academic nor aesthetic—but comic.

Comic imagination always fixes itself first on common things, it is concerned with the ordinary rather than the exotic, society rather than the solitary spirit in its romantic loneliness or isolation. The comic spirit is concerned with practical things, with the everyday world, and the voice of its conscience speaks of making ends meet, of getting along, and when inspired, of finding the amusement and delight in daily life, of finding the extraordinary hidden within the ordinary. This for Wallace Stevens is the task and challenge the human imagination must meet. It must

3

reveal the variations in perceiving a simple plum; it must attend the circuses of human reverie, wed thought to feeling, and, in accomplishing this, give life to all abstraction. It must make rich the poorest man who will but shape his dreams or look about, and measure wealth by all the landscapes to be seen, and measure human dignity by the pleasure music may bring to the ear.

The predominant quality of Stevens' verse—with its extensive vocabulary, metrical dexterity, and relationship of sense and sound—is eloquence. He is the master of two styles, one epigrammatic, eccentric, teasing; the other exalted and rhetorical in the manner of Wordsworth, in which his words have the ring of authority and command. His language is written partly for its own sake, although his rhetoric always suits the mood in which it is spoken. Besides the wide variety of sound effects and his use of colors as symbols, color and sound are used also in a more general way to evoke a mood or provide a sensual background for the flights of thought, as in "Domination of Black." Stevens' acute sense of color and sound becomes part of a larger awareness of the sensual as a principle, a force, and of physical life as the setting in which thought

and imagination thrive. Nowhere is this physical life more
vividly evoked than in the heavy air, the gurgle and crack,
of "Frogs Eat Butterflies. Snakes Eat Frogs. Hogs Eat
Snakes. Men Eat Hogs" (p. 78):

It is true that the rivers went nosing like swine,
Tugging at banks, until they seemed
Bland belly-sounds in somnolent troughs,

That the air was heavy with the breath of these swine,
The breath of turgid summer, and
Heavy with thunder's rattapallax,

That the man who erected this cabin, planted
This field, and tended it awhile,
Knew not the quirks of imagery,

That the hours of his indolent, arid days,
Grotesque with this nosing in banks,
This somnolence and rattapallax,

Seemed to suckle themselves on his arid being,
As the swine-like rivers suckled themselves
While they went seaward to the sea-mouths.

In Stevens' poetry we were always given an awareness of place. Even with such fundamental symbols as moon and sun the actual presence of the moon and the sun is always felt. The awareness of place, as in the feeling one has standing on the shore confronting the sublimity of the sea, is inevitably followed by the flow of speech, since a poem is part of a feeling, augmenting and inseparable from whatever it describes.

Wallace Stevens' verse has been called impersonal. It is true that his descriptive power is frequently objective, and it is also true that he does not present to his reader personal problems that consume his thought, yet to call him impersonal is misleading. Stevens' imagination is his most personal possession, and he presents its activity to us with vivid directness; we come to know the adroitness of his mind, touch what he touches, and see what he sees. There is feeling in Stevens' poetry although it rarely contains the voltage of passion. But must we make the mistake of confusing passion with personality? To learn of anguish let us turn to the pages of Yeats, but for philosophy as feeling, for nuances of perception, let us read Wallace Stevens. If we make a change in the usual description of Stevens, alter-

ing philosophic impersonality to read philosophic personality, then we will think of him more as he is.

What gives the illusion of impersonality is the tone of
irony that Stevens often employs; but this irony is part of
his character as a poet. It is not something he employs for
protection either from us or from himself. What strikes
him as ironic he describes through irony. Stevens is a
comic poet examining the world; much of it is lovely,
some of it is perplexing, and very often it is trivial, ironic
or humorous.

When Wallace Stevens uses irony or humor, it is his
manner of regarding his subject more seriously. "Le
Monocle de Mon Oncle" (p. 13) is a profoundly serious
poem, and yet not only is the title ironic, but so is much
within the poem. Its humor is turned against itself, not to
attack or destroy, but as a form of introspection. Language
is used self-consciously in this poem, calling attention to
itself and momentarily distracting from the poem's strictest sense. This is intentional. The monocled uncle is a
self-conscious person trying to reach beyond language and
beyond himself to an understanding of life. Looking at
the world through his monocle, the uncle may appear to

us affected, prissy, or having a single view. But we watch vision gradually supersede sight. The poem opens with a burst of affected, though lovely, language, and in a tone of mockery:

"Mother of heaven, regina of the clouds,
O sceptre of the sun, crown of the moon,
There is not nothing, no, no, never nothing,
Like the clashed edges of two words that kill."
And so I mocked her in magnificent measure.
Or was it that I mocked myself alone?

The uncle speaks of the clashed edges of words, and uses "mocked" twice. He is trying to get from the word to the thing itself; no wonder that he should be acutely conscious of the words he finds himself using:

The sea of spuming thought foists up again
The radiant bubble that she was. And then
A deep up-pouring from some saltier well
Within me, bursts its watery syllable.

Thought gives way to something deeper—feeling, and the "sea of spuming thought" is replaced by "some saltier well." There is both a powerful consciousness and self-consciousness working within this poem; the problem is their reconciliation. This reconciliation is achieved through humor and inner wit, the function of which is to translate individual feeling and perception into more general truth:

A red bird flies across the golden floor.
It is a red bird that seeks out his choir
Among the choirs of wind and wet and wing.
A torrent will fall from him when he finds.
Shall I uncrumple this much-crumpled thing?

The first four lines provide us with an evocative metaphor about the red bird which does not yield its meaning clearly. And so the uncle, as if in an aside, asks the rhetorical question, "Shall I uncrumple this much-crumpled thing?" and then goes on to "uncrumple" the metaphor:

I am a man of fortune greeting heirs;
For it has come that thus I greet the spring.

These choirs of welcome choir for me farewell.
No spring can follow past meridian.

The explanation does not replace the original lines, but adds to them while revealing the inner workings of the uncle's mind. He is serious, but at the same time witty—never sentimental—a man searching beyond his own convictions.

The uncle, considering his own and his wife's middle age, and recalling her youth, "the radiant bubble that she was," is nevertheless moved to discover an order in the vanishings of time:

If men at forty will be painting lakes
The ephemeral blues must merge for them in one,
The basic slate, the universal hue.
There is a substance in us that prevails.

This poem is constructed as a series of alternating perspectives: (1) The belief in a prevailing substance. (2) The observation of diminishings ("Before one merely reads to pass the time"), fallings off ("then amours shrink"), of

10

the rotting and death of things in time, with the accompanying awareness of approaching old age:

Our bloom is gone. We are the fruit thereof.
Two golden gourds distended on our vines,
Into the autumn weather, splashed with frost,
Distorted by hale fatness, turned grotesque.
We hang like warty squashes, streaked and rayed,
The laughing sky will see the two of us
Washed into rinds by rotting winter rains.

(3) The vision of death and birth as part of a single process:

The honey of heaven may or may not come,
But that of earth both comes and goes at once.

The ironic tone of the poem comes from the fact that we cannot settle on the single view or philosophy the monocle suggests. Life itself becomes an ineffable, fluttering thing, like the flight of birds, and we must finally accept it in this way.

11

A blue pigeon it is, that circles the blue sky,
On sidelong wing, around and round and round.
A white pigeon it is, that flutters to the ground,
Grown tired of flight. Like a dark rabbi, I
Observed, when young, the nature of mankind,
In lordly study. Every day, I found
Man proved a gobbet in my mincing world.
Like a rose rabbi, later, I pursued,
And still pursue, the origin and course
Of love, but until now I never knew
That fluttering things have so distinct a shade.

We notice that in this acceptance of "fluttering things" the
affectation of language and the ironic tone have disappeared. Although "the origin and course/ Of love" is not
yet known, though still pursued, the reconciliation of consciousness and self-consciousness has been completed, and
a harmony achieved.

In all of Stevens' nature poetry, sensuousness is inseparable from the mystery of life and death. The imagination, as our main source of moral and aesthetic wisdom,
never achieves any final vision, for it is a human thing,
itself replete with the mystery of mortality. In Stevens'

world the individual is never as large as his imagination. He does not fill the world with his deeds as does a tragic hero, but with thought and its concomitant feeling. His mind moves in the direction of theory and toward the comprehension of the general and abstract. The personalities which inhabit his poems are people whose thoughts, perceptions and ideas are the main sources of their character: the poet, rabbi, scholar, reader, hero, comedian, captain, and ephebe. A figure like the "fat girl," a symbol of nature's fruition, is entirely passive, only seen and never heard. Ultimately, the active characters form one— their author. And, like him, their predilections are for precise observation of objects and scenery, for general statements, and also like him they keep the distance of perspective from what they are watching.

Stevens' poetry is sensuous, refined and mental. There is little commitment to action, but rather to the life of the imagination. There is no tragic necessity. The characters are abstractions. The stage on which they move is the stage of the mind, not of the world, although its settings have the look of the world. Earth is seen as a still life in which a powerful energy, that of the imagination, lies hidden.

Moral responsibility is not dramatized as the result of guilt or crime. There is no deleterious human foible, and no atonement; action is the movement of the mind among images of possibility. What happens is never as important as what is revealed in the chambers of thought. But a mental attitude is always united with a state of feeling— not mere aesthetic sensation, but the feeling of things touched or seen.

Wallace Stevens is not so depressed as the rest of his generation; he is rather more pleased with life than disappointed. The imagination does not grow old, nor does the world it perceives. The irony, the humor, the self-satire, are means by which Stevens' comic imagination keeps the proper distance from things, even if they are his own ideas, and protects the poet from defining the world by his own passions. The comic eye is never fixed in one place too long. For Stevens, the sun, as the illuminating energy, is the central symbol of reality. It appears to regard everything equally, lighting all things as if there were a special way in which each speck within the universe needed lighting. "The sun, in clownish yellow, but not a clown." The sun, just as the comedian, dresses both itself and the world as if it were a clown, pretending that everything must be seen from without, because to see everything from within, though perhaps truer to the self, is certainly falser to the world. Tragedy moves our sight from the world into the individual; comedy, from the individual into society or some larger context.

In the comic work of art there is no fixed beginning, middle, end or even plot as there is in tragedy. Stevens' work does evolve, but dwells upon as much as it can within its reach of present time, affirming the immediate. Comedy does not make a point of time, but assumes it, and there is no single crisis, for time never runs out leaving a hero with just a moment in which he must cease speculating and must act. Plot and action are the opposites of time; they assume that time is limited and can be used up. The result of character is action, and the result of action is fate, but this is seen to be true only on the stage where the confining logic of time is emphasized. For in reality it is the tragic hero who is limited, and not time itself.

While action is momentary, thought, on the other hand, resembles time in that it has no ostensible end, and so it seems logical to find that thought and speech, not plot, character and action, form the primary medium of comedy. The comic hero never acts significantly because he never quite finishes talking, inquiring or considering. All the aspects of speech and meditation are to be found in Stevens' poetry: rhetoric, aside, aphorism, digression, and elegance, which show the comic pose to be as conscious about the way it sounds as it is about its subject. For speech is the main vehicle for manners, and since comedy always demands an adjustment to its society even when satirically criticizing it, and society is a structure of manners and law, comic expression becomes its own end and subject.

Stevens, like his clown-hero Crispin, imbued with the comic spirit, attempts the discovery of the unusual within the quotidian. This has always been true of Stevens from the earliest poetry through his last major poem—"An Ordinary Evening in New Haven." In "The Comedian as the Letter C," Crispin's development is from the self as center out to society and the world. Crispin marries, settles down, has four daughters, and accepts the social life; he moves from romanticist to realist. But he never becomes so serious that he forgets everything except what he is talking about; his life does not become the world's problem as it does for a tragic hero. His stress on manners and reason is balanced by his mocking diction and extravagant metaphors, not because he is bitter about the real world, "For realist, what is is what should be," but because he knows his relative place in it and knows his relative size.

Characters in comedy are not so acutely delineated in one sense as they are in tragedy, for they are seen from a detached perspective and tend to resemble one another, typifying an aspect of human life rather than a single personality. Unless we say the clown's mask is his face, we must agree that the clown represents more than himself. He is a prototype, an abstraction like Stevens' hero and poet.

Stevens' poetry often produces that silent laughter of the gracefully and profoundly humorous, the main sources of which are his irony, diction and satire. Comedy and laughter aim at correcting, and since it is expedient that this correction reach as many people as possible, comic observation instinctively proceeds toward the general. We immediately perceive that this truth is descriptive of Wallace Stevens' poetry; his abstraction of the hero includes us all. In the mirror of generalization we can be criticized without being destroyed, we can laugh at our own image and discover, that though it is ludicrous, we can still love the lines that etch its sorrows and its gaiety.

TWO

The Secular Mystery

We live in an old chaos of the sun,
Or old dependency of day and night,
Or island solitude, unsponsored, free,
Of that wide water, inescapable.

Art is the product of that human faculty, the imagination, which enables man to enjoy his own absurdity and suffering, enables him to dramatize it and, as it were, make something of it external to himself, something apart with its own independent existence. But the artist's imagination is different from that of the ordinary man only in degree of intensity or, perhaps, it is coupled with a talent or simply the commitment to be an artist. The point is that almost every man is capable of being aware that he is having an experience at the very moment he is actually caught up in it. Certainly, in retrospect, what has happened to him is the object of his meditation, almost as if he were watching it on a stage, as if he personally were disengaged from the action. Thus experience is not only the actions in which we are involved, through which we suffer gains and losses, but also the material of aesthetic awareness, the means toward knowledge. We might say that the object of experience is to know that we have experienced it; our sense of life, of reality, of purpose, comes only with this knowledge.

By an afflatus, however, the imagination realizes that there are experiences it has not known directly for itself, that others' experiences are different, and that the possibility for experience is infinite. The imagination then begins to conceive of experience beyond its own immediate life, it begins to see that its own knowledge of itself is incomplete, and that Life is greater than the most exalted tragedy of any single man, greater than any single issue or idea. This is Wallace Stevens' comic vision, comic because man is dwarfed by the infinitude of reality of which he is but a minute part, and this infinitude does not converge upon him as it does upon the tragic hero, presenting him with moral choice in which the gods have a stake or by which mankind stands or falls. It is a secular vision because Stevens sees *this* world as paradise and does not look beyond it, despite man's mortality and his pain of incompleteness and imperfection. It is a vision into mystery because knowledge is endless in a world of infinite reality, where to the senses and the imagination there is always possible a new revelation, a new delight, and an expansion of the very spirit and breath of life.

In "Sunday Morning" (justly come to be recognized as Stevens' masterpiece, though unjustly to the exclusion of later poems), we find a woman, sitting in "a sunny chair," meditating about life and considering the alternatives of religious and natural devotion. We see this woman mostly in silence, as if she appeared in a painting, and the voice of the poet expresses her contemplation for her. The reader joins with the poet in his speculations, and the poet, speaking almost as if he and the woman were of one mind, brings the reader into the intimacy of the scene, and the frame of the poem encloses him. In the comfort of repose, the woman's thoughts about the "ancient sacrifice" dissolve into an apprehension of the colors in her room, and her mind wanders back over "wide water"—through time —to ancient Palestine. Her devotion is troubled by a double sense of time: the dreamlike appeal of the past and the present appeal of sensuous perception and feeling.

In part II Stevens takes up the argument in favor of the richness of natural experience, of human moodiness and elation, questioning our faith in divinity because of the insubstantiality of its revelation: "Why should she give her bounty to the dead?/ What is divinity if it can come/ Only in silent shadows and in dreams?" And then Stevens goes on to express beautifully the sublimity of our human response to nature, suggesting that divinity cannot be known outside of life, but only within it (p. 67):

Shall she not find in comforts of the sun,
In pungent fruit and bright, green wings, or else
In any balm or beauty of the earth,
Things to be cherished like the thought of heaven?
Divinity must live within herself:
Passions of rain, or moods in falling snow;
Grievings in loneliness, or unsubdued
Elations when the forest blooms; gusty
Emotions on wet roads on autumn nights;
All pleasures and all pains, remembering
The bough of summer and the winter branch.
These are the measures destined for her soul.

The line "Divinity must live within herself" sounds like a kind of pantheism, but Stevens never talks about God; the word "divinity" is used metaphorically as a superlative to describe what is exalted in human feeling. But Stevens' secularism carried with it the full weight of religious conviction. He is being both sincere and literal when he finds in "beauty of the earth,/ Things to be cherished like the thought of heaven." It is perhaps Stevens' most central and appealing belief that Man cannot conceive of a paradise superior in bliss to that we experience in our own world, our ordinary lives. And it is the central paradox of our earthly paradise that it includes with its bliss, indeed, inextricable from it, both pain and evil, the "grievings in loneliness," the "winter branch" as well as the "summer bough."

The drama of this poem is in the testing of the idea of earth as paradise. Stevens does this by conjecturing about the meanings of their separation and about the literal and metaphorical possibilities of their coming together. In part III, for example, Stevens describes Jove not as a man, but as a deity who "had his inhuman birth./ No mother suckled him," and yet people thought of him as if he were a real human being: "He moved among us, as a muttering king,/ Magnificent, would move among his hinds." The image or idea of a deity, as man's imaginative proliferation of reality, becomes so much a part of our lives, that the imaginative and the real become one, and with this union we have the wedding of heaven and earth.

Man desires to believe in an infinite reality and to be in some touch with it; thus to bring heaven into contact with earth is his greatest wish, and Stevens dramatizes this idea by showing how the mythology—which tells of gods like Jove entering into the affairs of men—was superseded by the Christian belief in the incarnation of Christ: "Until our blood, commingling, virginal,/ With heaven, brought such requital to desire/ The very hinds discerned it, in a star." With the assumption that in our contemporary world we have no myth to unite heaven with earth, Stevens asks whether our imaginations will fail to bring about such a marriage: "Shall our blood fail? Or shall it come to be/ The blood of paradise?" And after this moving inquiry Stevens makes his statement of a myth for our time, the idea of earth as heaven. This idea once triumphant, the sky would then cease to be an image of the

separation of heaven and earth and would become part
of the bounty of mortal aspiration and feeling:

The sky will be much friendlier then than now,
A part of labor and a part of pain,
And next in glory to enduring love,
Not this dividing and indifferent blue.

   With the exposition of the idea of earth as paradise completed, Stevens in part IV returns us to the woman whose
sense of the ephemeral quality of earthly beatitude sets
the poet to further speculation:

She says, "I am content when wakened birds,
Before they fly, test the reality
Of misty fields, by their sweet questionings;
But when the birds are gone, and their warm fields
Return no more, where, then, is paradise?"

And Stevens in answering, as if the woman were a voice
in a dialogue within his own mind, makes these points:
while nature is ephemeral it is always continuing and
being renewed; spring passes only in its time to return to

spring; personal memory and memory which becomes poetry retain the past; and our desires for the beauties of earthly paradise never leave us. These things prevail, and there is nothing, Stevens argues

> . . . that has endured
> As April's green endures; or will endure
> Like her remembrance of awakened birds,
> Of her desire for June and evening, tipped
> By the consummation of the swallow's wings.

The woman, feeling the beauty of earthly things in their continuity, nevertheless expresses the sentiment in part V that " 'in contentment I still feel/ The need of some imperishable bliss.' " And to this statement Stevens brings the full weight of the paradox on which the myth of an earthly paradise depends: "Death is the mother of beauty." Without death, we would take no passionate pleasure in the world, we would not feel its sensuousness, for there is no necessity or compulsion to possess that which is always there and which does not change. So Stevens can say of death that

> . . . Although she strews the leaves
> Of sure obliteration on our paths,
> The path sick sorrow took, the many paths
> Where triumph rang its brassy phrase, or love
> Whispered a little out of tenderness,
> She makes the willow shiver in the sun
> For maidens who were wont to sit and gaze
> Upon the grass, relinquished to their feet.
> She causes boys to pile new plums and pears
> On disregarded plate. The maidens taste
> And stray impassioned in the littering leaves.

Having expressed the necessity for death in an earthly paradise, Stevens attempts in part VI to dramatize this idea further by considering what a heavenly paradise where there is no death would be like. But immediately the idea is seen to be absurd: "Does ripe fruit never fall? Or do the boughs/ Hang always heavy in that perfect sky,/ Unchanging . . . ?" The very idea of ripeness is inseparable from the idea of change. And in the magnificently touching line, "Alas, that they should wear our colors there," Stevens communicates the fullness of his commitment to earth and articulates the conviction that the pleasures we know, "our colors," are endemic to the round of mortal life. Death is not the threshold to another world, a greater paradise, but has its meaning only in relation to us here, and from this relationship comes the infiniteness of the reality that sensuously encloses us, so that Stevens can say: "Death is the mother of beauty, mystical,/ Within whose burning bosom we devise/ Our earthly mothers waiting, sleeplessly."

It is perhaps difficult to know just how to regard the opening lines of part VII:

Supple and turbulent, a ring of men
Shall chant in orgy on a summer morn
Their boisterous devotion to the sun,
Not as a god, but as a god might be,
Naked among them, like a savage source.

Does Stevens mean this literally, does he imagine himself as one of the men participating spontaneously in this ritual of worshiping the sun as a symbol for the life force or for reality? It seems to me that Stevens means just what he says, and that this part is not a break in the directness and literalness of the poem. The rituals of any belief to which we do not give our credence seem absurd to us, and we are unable to picture ourselves participating in them without painful self-consciousness. Because of the sophistication of contemporary society, it is difficult to feel any commitment deeply, and certainly it is difficult to communicate the deep feelings we do have. But Stevens is saying that we can grow beyond this, and that we do have something to believe in with a passionate devotion—Reality, and the Imagination that names and reveals it, in the way that men have always named their gods.

To believe this with Stevens' conviction is to become innocent, to see the world as wonder, as "mystical," and to enter into its worship with a childlike freedom and enthusiasm. And in the worship there "shall be a chant of paradise," for men will be affirming without reservation and doubt the fact of their mortality and the sensuous beauty that greets them where they go: "They shall know well the heavenly fellowship/ Of men that perish and of summer morn."

Returning to the meditation of the woman in the last stanza, Stevens tells us that in her dreamlike invocation of the past (the imagery here as in part I is "water without sound") the woman hears "A voice that cries, 'The tomb in Palestine/ Is not the porch of spirits lingering./ It is the grave of Jesus, where he lay.'" With these lines we have a rejection of the supernatural, of Jesus as the Christ, and we feel a compassion for the drama of the man Jesus. At this point we are left only with earth in its "island solitude," and its endless history of death and of birth; for it is out of this history that we come and through its continuity that we move. Man's destiny and man's will are his own, and perhaps the greatest attribute of an earthly paradise is the freedom it allows:

We live in an old chaos of the sun,
Or old dependency of day and night,
Or island solitude, unsponsored, free,
Of that wide water, inescapable.

The juxtaposition here of "unsponsored" and "free" seems a touch of genius in which Stevens has concentrated volumes of theology into two words. Man is free, Stevens argues, because he is on his own, because he is acting out his own will and not the will of a deity greater than himself. Stevens cuts through all the paradoxes which try to reconcile God's foreknowledge with man's free will, divine law with freedom of choice, to the central mystery of his secular world: death as the mother of beauty, and change which gives to reality an infinitude of possibilities for imaginative and sensuous experience:

Deer walk upon our mountains, and the quail
Whistle about us their spontaneous cries;
Sweet berries ripen in the wilderness;
And, in the isolation of the sky,
At evening, casual flocks of pigeons make
Ambiguous undulations as they sink,
Downward to darkness on extended wings.

This poem is about incarnation, without which no idea, essence or spirit has reality. It is about Jove as "He moved among us, as a muttering king"; it is about Christ only in his incarnation as Jesus; and it is about the incarnation of the idea of this world as paradise. For in the "old chaos of the sun," in nature, we can actually worship the sensuous forms of an infinite, changing reality. And as the pigeons descend in the sky, like the spiritual dove given shape, they make "ambiguous undulations," for their reality is no single thing, though it is circumscribed by "darkness."

"Esthétique du Mal" can profitably be read as a sequel to "Sunday Morning," for not only is it like "Sunday Morning" in form and style but it picks up the question of whether earth can be a paradise where the "ambiguous undulations" of "Sunday Morning" and the "fluttering things" of "Le Monocle de Mon Oncle" leave off. Having accepted, rather embraced, death and mutability in the earlier poem, Stevens goes on in "Esthétique du Mal" (p. 313) to consider the place of evil and pain in his paradise on earth. As the title suggests, evil becomes a question of aesthetics, and ultimately serves an aesthetic end. The poem begins with a man sitting in his room in Naples, "reading paragraphs/ On the sublime," much as the woman in "Sunday Morning" was enjoying her coffee and oranges— for they are both concerned first with pleasure. As he reads, Stevens says, "It was pleasant to be sitting there," and yet, in comfort, the man's thoughts focus upon images of pain, as those of the woman turned to thoughts of death. Stevens makes the same use of the man in this poem as of the woman in the earlier one; they are figures through whom he can express his own meditations and whom he can use as part of the dialectic of his own thinking.

It is appropriate that the protagonist of the poem is reading about the sublime and thinking about Vesuvius, for the sublime is that strange mixture of beauty and terror, bliss and pain, that causes an ecstasy of wonder and awe, revealing for an instant the mystery of the universe. "Pain is human," Stevens says, and without its presence no feeling at all is possible:

Except for us, Vesuvius might consume
In solid fire the utmost earth and know
No pain (ignoring the cocks that crow us up
To die). This is a part of the sublime
From which we shrink. And yet, except for us,
The total past felt nothing when destroyed.

It is not Vesuvius that knows pain, that mourns the destruction of a man, a city, an age; it is we who know

Vesuvius as an image of pain. Our pain is a knowledge, a sense of ourselves inseparable from our sense of the past. If to be in paradise is to have a consciousness of the sublime, there must be change and therefore death, and therefore pain as well as bliss.

The idea of pain being inextricable from our sense of time and mutability, and from our sensuous experience of things, encourages our acceptance of earth in its totality. This is the intent of "Esthétique du Mal," and this theme is examined in a series of stanzas which are discursive and not so closely tied together as those of "Sunday Morning." Since Stevens' argument is not consecutive and does not unfold in logical steps, but is rather a variety of dramatizations of a theme, it is not necessary to examine the poem strictly stanza by stanza.

To understand why this earthly paradise does not ever seem to be fixed, does not become like the ripe fruit in a heavenly paradise that never falls, one must understand the imagination that conceives this paradise. The earth-as-paradise is of course an imagined thing, but this is not to say that it is not real, not true. It is an approach to the truth, and Stevens never forgets this, for he knows that the Truth is something that exceeds the statements his imagination can make about it. There is an infinite reality that his imagination believes in, but it can be only partially known. Yet the imagination does not stop contented with its present statements, its fine and articulate descriptions, but is constantly aware of new possibilities for description which reflect part of the reality it had not previously taken into account. The protagonist of this poem, contemplating the meaning of the sublime and its essential constituent—pain—realizes that there is something his "meditation never quite achieved." And at that instant, Stevens tells us:

The moon rose up as if it had escaped
His meditation. It evaded his mind.
It was part of a supremacy always
Above him. The moon was always free from him,
As night was free from him. The shadow touched
Or merely seemed to touch him as he spoke
A kind of elegy he found in space . . .

The moon, his imagination, makes its presence felt even beyond his meditation. It is the imagination that sees pain not as a thing in itself but as part of a reality which includes it. Thus, as part of the sublime, pain is not what it seems at first. The imagination, able to know this, is always free, for it is a consciousness disinterested in a man's personal pain. And the "elegy" the man finds in space is the endless song of the imagination singing of mutability and pain, for that is also to sing of paradise. It is pain aware only of itself as pain, about which Stevens says: "It does not regard/ This freedom, this supremacy, and in/ Its own hallucination never sees/ How that which rejects it saves it in the end." The "hallucination" of pain is that it does not see beyond itself into the complex richness of the sublime, into the paradox of earthly paradise that properly sees earth as complete in itself and makes pain "indifferent to the sky," so that it remains part of the sublime and is, after all, saved.

The acceptance of pain, the imagination's song, is the theme Stevens sings through the mind of the man meditating on the sublime whose "firm stanzas hang like hives in hell/ Or what hell was, since now both heaven and hell/ Are one, and here." If it were regarded only as pain, Stevens says, "The fault lies with an over-human god,/ Who by sympathy has made himself a man." But Stevens does not want his sympathy, indeed, he wants nothing to alter the reality of earth, and says of the god "If only he would not pity us so much,/ Weaken our fate," because a "too human god" is "self-pity's kin." The world as it is is how Stevens wants it:

It seems as if the honey of common summer
Might be enough, as if the golden combs
Were part of a sustenance itself enough,

As if hell, so modified, had disappeared,
As if pain, no longer satanic mimicry,
Could be borne, as if we were sure to find our way.

To talk about pain, mutability and death in the light of such a belief as original sin, as disobedience to divine will, as the violating of some cosmic moral law, is to assume a tragic perspective of human history. To talk about human evil in a satirical or bitingly critical manner is to assume a belief in the possibility of social progress and, at least, relative human perfectibility. But to accept the world as it is, and in this acceptance to see it joyfully, is to possess, as Stevens does, a comic vision. Change, according to this vision, does not lead toward a goal, a destination, a state of human perfection, but continues to renew that which already is. There is a lightness to such a philosophy, and this lightness is often reflected in Stevens' style, even in a poem about pain. Stevens speaks of the "Spaniard of the rose" who

>   . . . rescued the rose
> From nature, each time he saw it, making it,
> As he saw it, exist in his own especial eye.
> Can we conceive of him as rescuing less,
> As muffing the mistress for her several maids . . . ?

Here he is exploring the idea of change, and is thinking of it as the infinite reality of the rose to which the perceiver always responds freshly, bringing to its reality the illuminating power of his imagination. But the tone is teasing; an aesthetic, not a moral, question is involved. The mandate to live imaginatively, constantly to see the rose as something new, is in the name of pleasure, not in the name of law. The "Spaniard" knows that he is in paradise, in a garden where the sight of a rose will never be dull and will never cloy, for he is a hero of the imagination. His opposite, "the genius of misfortune," sees his own troubles, his own pain, mirrored in the world's image; he sees not the rose but his sorrow in the rose, for he possesses "that evil in the self, from which/ In desperate hallow, rugged gesture, fault/ Falls out on everything."

Stevens has rejected the pity that an "over-human god" would feel for mankind and asks that "all true sympathizers come,/ Without the inventions of sorrow," for to feel self-pity is to fail to see the world as it is—a mortal world of change which, by a paradox conceived by the imagination, seems to have the conditions of paradise. Thus, Stevens says, "we forego/ Lament, willingly forfeit the ai-ai." The horror in the world does not define it. In abstraction, from the distance of an aesthetic perspective, Stevens can see the essence of loveliness in the necessary defeat of "the soldier of time," a soldier whose image includes us all:

How red the rose that is the soldier's wound,
The wounds of many soldiers, the wounds of all
The soldiers that have fallen, red in blood,
The soldier of time grown deathless in great size.

. . . . .

The shadows of his fellows ring him round
In the high night, the summer breathes for them
Its fragrance, a heavy somnolence, and for him,
For the soldier of time, it breathes a summer sleep,

In which his wound is good because life was.

How are we to take this? How far can Stevens extend his
point? Though we may be willing to grant that war,
death and pain are part of a larger reality, perhaps even
that they are somehow a necessary part of paradise, nevertheless, is there not an immediacy, an actuality to pain
that Stevens overlooks? Yet, when he says, "That he might
suffer or that/ He might die was the innocence of living,"
we are disabused of any feeling that there is a false complacency in Stevens' vision of earthly paradise. Stevens

himself is aware of the danger of such a complacency, and he comments on the above statement, saying that it "Disentangled him from sleek ensolacings."

With part XI we read Stevens' most direct, seemingly least paradoxical, statement about pain:

Life is a bitter aspic. We are not
At the centre of a diamond. At dawn,
The paratroopers fall and as they fall
They mow the lawn. A vessel sinks in waves
Of people, as big bell-billows from its bell
Bell-bellow in the village steeple. Violets,
Great tufts, spring up from buried houses
Of poor, dishonest people, for whom the steeple,
Long since, rang out farewell, farewell, farewell.

The subjects of his imagery are grim: war, drowning; he strips away the sentiment we are inclined to feel about poor people, making human dishonesty seem its most ignominious. And yet the imagery itself is graceful and lovely. The incongruity here of subject and style dramatizes subtly the point Stevens wants to make, and following the above passage, he then makes his point explicit in one marvelous couplet: "Natives of poverty, children of malheur,/ The gaiety of language is our seigneur." Language, the primary manifestation of imagination, possesses a gaiety of its own, so that in describing the world we transform it partly into our own image. This transformation is not a falsification of reality. When we say war is terrible, are we not describing it here, too, in our own image? Do not all events have reality only in reference to the consciousness that perceives those events? Stevens, in his own defense, says: "A man of bitter appetite despises/ A well-made scene in which paratroopers/ Select adieux." Reality, according to Stevens, does not impose itself upon us, so that wisdom is a condition of perfect passivity; rather reality presents itself as half completed until shaped into an order, a "well-made scene," by the imagination.

Stevens illustrates this interdependence of reality and imagination by speaking of the former as the "peopled" world, and the latter as the "unpeopled." The protagonist of the poem, considering both, finds that

. . . in the peopled world, there is,
Besides the people, his knowledge of them. In
The unpeopled, there is his knowledge of himself.
Which is more desperate in the moments when
The will demands that what he thinks be true?

Is it himself in them that he knows or they
In him? If it is himself in them, they have
No secret from him. If it is they in him,
He has no secret from them.

To follow this logic is to see that we cannot know one world without the other, that one cannot exist without the other, and therefore, "This knowledge/ Of them and of himself destroys both worlds,/ Except when he escapes from it." But to escape from this knowledge is to be totally isolated from experience, "To be/ Alone." And only in a "world without knowledge . . . there is no pain." For those who suffer, since we do live in a world of knowledge, as, for example, when "one life is a punishment/ For another, as the son's life for the father's," there is, as part of their knowledge, a consolation, an awareness that takes them outside of themselves and outside of their own suffering: They, too, may know, as Stevens tells us, that such punishment "concerns the secondary characters./ It is a fragmentary tragedy/ Within the universal whole." All men as individuals are "secondary characters," for it is only the full reality of the two worlds in one that is primary, and since each individual partakes of it, has knowledge of it, he may exist beyond his own pain.

Stevens argues that to feel one emotion, such as pain, in a world of emotions is to see pain falsely and to see the world falsely; one must, rather, have a sense of oneself as part of the whole. If reality were anything less than the whole, and if the whole were anything less than infinite, this world could not be a paradise. This belief is so important to Stevens that, having shown how an emotion is misunderstood when seen in isolation, he goes on to show us how an idea is abused when held to the exclusion of other ideas. Stevens repeats the words spoken about Konstantinov, the revolutionary: " 'I followed his argument/ With the blank uneasiness which one might feel/ In the presence of a logical lunatic.' " "Revolution," Stevens then says, "is the affair of logical lunatics." Revolutionists may be logical in their deductions from a premise, but their

lunacy consists in their insistence upon that premise, as if
the truth were so simple a thing that one might reach it by
a sustained logic:

One might meet Konstantinov, who would interrupt
With his lunacy. He would not be aware of the lake.
He would be the lunatic of one idea
In a world of ideas, who would have all the people
Live, work, suffer and die in that idea
In a world of ideas. He would not be aware of the clouds,
Lighting the martyrs of logic with white fire.
His extreme of logic would be illogical.

It is touching that Stevens says, "He would not be aware
of the lake," "He would not be aware of the clouds,"
rather than to say he would not be aware of the merits of
socialism or of capitalism. Not that this wouldn't be true,
but Stevens wishes to emphasize the physical world the
logical lunatic has forgotten, for it is our sensuous experience of things, the aesthetics of reality, that makes earth
a paradise in which the point of existence lies in the pleasure of existence, and in the awareness of that pleasure.

Although for Stevens, "The greatest poverty is not to live/ In a physical world," nevertheless, the physical world is not cut off from the imaginative, the metaphysical; and so Stevens, to illustrate this idea of the unity of physical and metaphysical as occurring only on earth, invents the hypothesis that after this life "the non-physical people, in paradise,/ Itself non-physical, may, by chance, observe/ The green corn gleaming and experience/ The minor of what we feel." They cannot bring to experience the richness of both the sensuous and the imaginative, and therefore know only the "minor" of our feelings for whom the "green corn gleams and the metaphysicals/ Lie sprawling in majors of the August heat." The "majors" of our experience may exist with "paradise unknown," for we are not "non-physical people," but Stevens' irony has reversed the formal, metaphorical sense of paradise and made the word fit the literal description of earth. It is this description of earth-as-paradise then that "is the thesis scrivened in delight,/ The reverberating psalm, the right chorale." As in "Sunday Morning," Stevens proposes a ritual: a psalm, a chorale, as the necessary expression for his belief, and concludes his poem in an elegiac tone of pleasure

and delight, reconciled to pain and evil, singing of the
secular mystery:

One might have thought of sight, but who could think
Of what it sees, for all the ill it sees?
Speech found the ear, for all the evil sound,
But the dark italics it could not propound.
And out of what one sees and hears and out
Of what one feels, who could have thought to make
So many selves, so many sensuous worlds,
As if the air, the mid-day air, was swarming
With the metaphysical changes that occur,
Merely in living as and where we live.

THREE

Resemblance and Correspondence: The Unity of Person and Place

○   The mind is the terriblest force in the world.

              The eye's plain version is a thing apart,
              The vulgate of experience.

Wallace Stevens is a philosopher as well as a connoisseur of physical sensations and perceptions, and out of his interest in objects and facts he explores the questions of epistemology; and from his interest in the human imagination he searches out the meanings open to metaphysical speculation. His philosophy—or rather his way of making a philosophical inquiry—is implicit in his earliest poetry in *Harmonium* and continues to be found throughout all his work, tending to become more explicit in *Transport to Summer, The Auroras of Autumn,* and the last poems. But Stevens never merely philosophizes, using the form of verse as a temptation; he presents the drama of the mind as it manipulates the details of perception; he shows us how the mind receives and resists the world, and teaches us that thought has its own emotions. What is it like to have an idea? What is it like to perceive things and to know that one is perceiving them, and to be aware that this knowing becomes part of the perceiving? To these questions Wallace Stevens brings the wisdom of his imagination. And the theory that is a product of this inquiry is at the heart of Stevens' poetry.

The world Wallace Stevens describes to us is richly alive with a wonder of textures, colors, shadings, big and little things, perfumes, musical and natural sounds, strange shapes and pleasing contours; he titillates our senses into that heightened activity of acute consciousness, and from this consciousness emerges an understanding of reality as a unified structure of correspondences and resemblances. Nevertheless, things as we see them are not the starting point for Stevens. He postulates an independent body of images, first things, things "as they are." The first moment of our immediate perception comes closest to the object, "things as they are," for in that instant we have not yet imposed ourselves, but see the object itself. The transition of the object into the percipient's concept begins another movement which leads into a new order of correspondences, and a new attitude toward the object. But the first allegiance of the artist, according to Stevens, is to the world as it exists independent of man's thinking.

> "But play, you must,
> A tune beyond us, yet ourselves,
>
> A tune upon the blue guitar
> Of things exactly as they are."

In the long poem "The Man with the Blue Guitar" (p. 165), which deals specifically with the artist, his craft and his audience, Stevens associates the color blue with the guitar as a symbol of the imagination in contrast to the color green which symbolizes "things as they are." "The day was green," we are told in the first couplet, and "things as they are" become "things as they seem" when rendered on the guitar. But it is *perception* out of which knowledge may grow. One must first see the world to understand it. "In my room, the world is beyond my understanding;/ But when I walk I see that it consists of three or/ Four hills and a cloud." Stevens looks about him, and this is his beginning; he believes in a real world whose reality includes him as an object, and also includes his imaginative faculty.

An object loses its independence as it becomes involved in the particular history of the perceiving mind, and we must begin to speak of the apprehension of this object, for it is seen within a particular psychological and aesthetic reference. From this point on, the higher consciousness comes into play in the further ordering of the apperception. The relationship between the newly perceived object and other remembered objects forms a correspondence, and thus is evolved a complex organization, a conception. It is the discovery and succeeding organization of resemblances and correspondences that for Stevens is the work of poetry, and in this activity lies his most profound pleasure which is also the pleasure of improvisation, of "merely circulating."

In the continual ordering of the ambient flow of images, all life tends to become literature. There are three types of relationships which this ordering produces, and in each case we observe the process of perception becoming apperception and culminating in conception. *Resemblance* is the discovered relationship between external objects. The

most simple form of resemblance is seen in "Tattoo"
(p. 81) and "Thirteen Ways of Looking at a Blackbird"
(p. 94):

The light is like a spider.
It crawls over the water.
It crawls over the edges of the snow.

The river is moving.
The blackbird must be flying.

In "Anecdote of the Jar" (p. 76) there is a more complex
resemblance:

I placed a jar in Tennessee,
And round it was, upon a hill,
It made the slovenly wilderness
Surround that hill.

The jar and the hill are not equal to each other although
they have a partial similarity, but in grouping them together by means of this similarity they take on a new
quality. They become circles within the larger circle of
the "slovenly wilderness," exerting a pressure that shapes

things into a geometric figuration. All three are now brought together by a resemblance: the larger to the smaller circles. The wilderness can now be seen for the first time, for we have discovered its shape. No longer is it "slovenly" in a perceptual chaos: "The wilderness rose up to it,/ And sprawled around, no longer wild."

The more complex resemblance is the "metaphor," which is a description of something in terms of something else that in immediate perception it does not resemble. The metaphor seeks out a hidden similarity, it reveals the quality of things as in "The Wind Shifts" (p. 83):

This is how the wind shifts:
Like the thoughts of an old human,
Who still thinks eagerly
And despairingly.
The wind shifts like this:
Like a human without illusions,
Who still feels irrational things within her.
The wind shifts like this:
Like humans approaching proudly,
Like humans approaching angrily.

This is how the wind shifts:
Like a human, heavy and heavy,
Who does not care.

It is not readily apparent that the shifting of the wind and
the alternation of human passions resemble one another,
but the suggestion takes hold and we come to see, under
the guidance of the poet's imagination, that it is true. We
see the gusto and windiness of human emotion, and man
and wind become inseparable in their mutual resemblance.
In discovering this unity Stevens shows his reader how
the inner and outer worlds are bound together by a secret tie.

The relationship of the internal and the external, of
inner feeling and outer fact, is a "correspondence." As
resemblances are similarities between externals, correspondences are similarities between states of mind and
material phenomena. Inasmuch as thought concerning an
object expresses something about that object, the discovery
of correspondences releases the forms of expression that
physical reality implies, and enables the poet to merge

with the world he finds enclosing him in the new world
of his poem:

A poem is a particular of life thought of for so long that
one's thought has become an inseparable part of it or a
particular of life so intensely felt that the feeling has
entered into it. (*Nec. Ang.*, p. 65)

The inner weather of the mind and the outer weather of
the world are related and interdependent. One cannot exist without the other, although as abstractions we can imagine them apart, as a mind that receives and records, and
as matter that is apprehended according to its material
properties. The mind, of course, is not merely passive to
outer impressions, but reflects the hungers and motiva-
tions of the body as well as its own subjective aspirations,
and our abstraction does not take this into account. But
even allowing for this simplification, we discover that the
mind has an imaginative component, and in addition to
seeing properties like size and color, it recognizes prin-
ciples of organization, of form, and qualities such as
beauty. This quality of beauty cannot be simply located in

either the mind or in the object, for it exists only in the meeting of the two, and so it becomes apparent that the meeting of these two worlds creates a third, a world of correspondences. Wallace Stevens' search for correspondences is thus an exploration for the possible as part of the real. Intuition is the discovery of such possibility, and expression therefore is not merely the mirror of reality but also its extension. Sensation alone records only an aspect of what it responds to, while the imagination, according to the principle by which it lives, knows that every finite thing has an infinite existence.

The architecture of reality, therefore, is seen by Stevens as a structure of infinite correspondences and resemblances, and since reality is not static, but dynamic, and since the world is still in the process of being created, it must be the function of the imagination to discover correspondences, knowing that "in some sense all things resemble each other" (*Nec. Ang.,* p. 71). Such discovery is the highest satisfaction for man, according to Stevens, whose greatest desire is for order.

The poet leads the quest for the knowledge of resemblances in a struggle against chaos. Order, then, is not merely faithfulness to sense data, but also the organization of facts in relation to each other and to the perceiver. Without this order human aspiration is not able to achieve satisfaction, since, in chaos, it would be impossible for desire to distinguish the desirable object. The divorce between desire and the object of desire is the condition of chaos as in "Chaos in Motion and Not in Motion" (p. 357), where Stevens describes the "turbulent Schlemihl" who "Has lost the whole in which he was contained,/ Knows desire without an object of desire,/ All mind and violence and nothing felt." Chaos is the word Stevens chooses to describe the feeling of being lost in a totally subjective emotion. Home is the place where one understands the routine, knows the secret rhythms of family activity and communication, and feels the fullness of the presence of familiar objects. It is this intimacy that Stevens seeks to have with the world, and it is the sense of order the poet achieves that makes this intimacy possible.

Such poems as "Theory" (p. 86) illustrate Stevens' attempt to discover the relationship between himself and the world about him:

I am what is around me.

Women understand this.
One is not duchess
A hundred yards from a carriage.

The beginning of a definition of a man lies in the scene
that encloses him. In "Six Significant Landscapes" (p. 73),
for example, the clothing functions as metaphor for the
man:

Rationalists, wearing square hats,
Think, in square rooms,
Looking at the floor,
Looking at the ceiling.
They confine themselves
To right-angled triangles.
If they tried rhomboids,
Cones, waving lines, ellipses—
As, for example, the ellipse of the half moon—
Rationalists would wear sombreros.

Each scene, each place, with its particular characteristics,
its climate, its coloring, its fields or buildings, gives shape

to the personalities of the men and women who live there. In "Anecdote of Men by the Thousand" (p. 51):

The soul, he said, is composed
Of the external world.

There are men of the East, he said,
Who are the East.
There are men of a province
Who are that province.
There are men of a valley
Who are that valley.

. . . . .

The dress of a woman of Lhassa,
In its place,
Is an invisible element of that place
Made visible.

Every man in his uniqueness expresses the invisible elements of his place; and place, in its uniqueness, expresses the invisible elements within its residents. Stevens' discovered correspondences reveal something about ourselves and about the world, but how do we know when we have discovered a true resemblance or correspondence? Does it continue to exist after the thought is past or after our reading of a poem, or does it somehow fade away, leaving us with nothing but a vague remembrance and a sense of illusion?

Stevens is able to achieve an order out of a chaos of objects, and is able to reveal man's subtle relationship to this order. It is as if there were something the eye *had* to see and something the ear *had* to hear, and Stevens, in ordering his world, has learned how to find them out. But the matter does not even rest here. For the object of the searching mind is not only the world, but itself. In its imaginative functioning it fulfills itself, and at the same time it is confronted by its own limitation. The quality of a perceived object, in turn, becomes part of the quality of the perceiving imagination. Stevens says "Every image is a restatement of the subject of the image in the terms of an attitude" (*Nec. Ang.*, p. 128). This restatement, as in the writing of a poem, uncovers the correspondences between the subjective and objective worlds, and leads to the desired unity of person and place, resolving the apparent dichotomy between "things as they are" as known to the perfect perceptual eye and things as they are changed by the imagination.

This resolution of person and place into a unity, however, is only momentary. Once made, it is not then fixed for time to come, but is as fleeting as time itself. Each moment requires a new resolution, and the imagination must continually exert its power to see the world freshly. In the remarkable poem "The Snow Man" (p. 9) Stevens dramatizes the action of a mind as it becomes one with the scene it perceives, and at that instant, the mind having ceased to bring something of itself to the scene, the scene then ceases to exist fully.

One must have a mind of winter
To regard the frost and the boughs
Of the pine-trees crusted with snow;

And have been cold a long time
To behold the junipers shagged with ice,
The spruces rough in the distant glitter

Of the January sun; and not to think
Of any misery in the sound of the wind,
In the sound of a few leaves,

Which is the sound of the land
Full of the same wind
That is blowing in the same bare place

For the listener, who listens in the snow,
And, nothing himself, beholds
Nothing that is not there and the nothing that is.

We, with the "one" of the poem, begin by watching the
winter scene while in our mind the connotations of misery
and cold brought forth by the scene are stirring. But gradually, almost imperceptibly, we are divested of whatever
it is that distinguishes us from the snow man. We become
the snow man, and we see the winter world through his
eyes of coal, and we know the cold without the thoughts
of human discomfort. To perceive the winter scene truly,
we must have the mind of the snow man, until correspondence becomes identification. Then we see with the
sharpest eye the images of winter: "pine-trees crusted with
snow," "junipers shagged with ice," "spruces rough in the
distant glitter/ Of the January sun." We hear with the
acutest ear the cold sibilants evoking the sense of barrenness and monotony: "sound of the wind," "sound of a few

leaves," "sound of the land," "same wind," "same bare place," "For the listener, who listens in the snow." The "one" with whom the reader has identified himself has now become "the listener, who listens in the snow"; he has become the snow man, and he knows winter with a mind of winter, knows it in its strictest reality, stripped of all imagination and human feeling. But at that point when he sees the winter scene reduced to absolute fact, as the object not of the mind, but of the perfect perceptual eye that sees "nothing that is not there," then the scene, devoid of its imaginative correspondences, has become "the nothing that is."

In the poem "Life Is Motion" (p. 83) we witness, rather than participate in, a correspondence of person and place, and we see how they are unified:

In Oklahoma,
Bonnie and Josie,
Dressed in calico,
Danced around a stump.
They cried,
"Ohoyaho,
Ohoo." . . .

Celebrating the marriage
Of flesh and air.

The names, "Bonnie and Josie," the place "Oklahoma,"
and the dress, "calico," are all obviously related. The title
of the poem suggests the antithesis of the dancing "Bonnie
and Josie" and the static "stump," an antithesis between
life and death. The stump is not only placed in the center
of the scene, but also in the center of the poem (there are
eleven words both before and after "stump"). "Bonnie
and Josie" are part of the life that surrounds the stump of
death, and they are joined with this life, "the marriage/
Of flesh and air." Even their cry sounds like the wind and
ameliorates the analogy that likens them to the air. This
poem completes a correspondence of inner and outer reality as well as the unification of its limited world.

If, for a moment, we can imagine an abstract world
where absolutes exist and where there is a single relationship between perceiver and perceived, then we can understand the problem Stevens poses as to how this relationship can change when seen by the imagination. Reality,
based on the most rigid discipline of accurate perception,

is changed by the imagination into a fuller reality. These elaborations do not negate the strictest reality, but discover within it new relationships. Even the fullest reality must, in time, return to the strict discipline of perception, and every fullness, though ephemeral, in its moment of flourishing is nonetheless real.

In "A Rabbit as King of the Ghosts" (p. 209) a rabbit is doing the imagining, and through his eyes we watch the changing of his world in which the most important object is the cat. But at the same time that we see through the eyes of the rabbit we are outside the poem and can see both the rabbit and the cat change, so that a new correspondence takes place between them:

The difficulty to think at the end of day,
When the shapeless shadow covers the sun
And nothing is left except light on your fur—

There was the cat slopping its milk all day,
Fat cat, red tongue, green mind, white milk
And August the most peaceful month.

To be, in the grass, in the peacefullest time,
Without that monument of cat,
The cat forgotten in the moon;

And to feel that the light is a rabbit-light,
In which everything is meant for you
And nothing need be explained;

Then there is nothing to think of. It comes of itself;
And east rushes west and west rushes down,
No matter. The grass is full

And full of yourself. The trees around are for you,
The whole of the wideness of night is for you,
A self that touches all edges,

You become a self that fills the four corners of night.
The red cat hides away in the fur-light
And there you are humped high, humped up,

You are humped higher and higher, black as stone—
You sit with your head like a carving in space
And the little green cat is a bug in the grass.

Stevens' use of the word "ghost" in the title suggests a spirit as part of the imagination the rabbit embodies. Through the proliferation of his thought, the rabbit almost expunges the world in a momentary realization of his own largeness. In spite of "The difficulty to think at the end of day" (because the accurate light of the sun has impressed us with things as they appear to the eye), the light on the rabbit's fur becomes the moonlight on the rabbit's fur, which, in turn, becomes the imaginative light of the rabbit's mind. We see the cat as it is "slopping its milk" and are able to think about it because we are in a peaceful month of summer (a time when the earth extends itself with an abundance of fecund images). We observed earlier that the color green is used to suggest "things as they are," the strictest reality. The cat in this poem, because of its "green mind," cannot conceive of the rabbit's potential largeness, and does not lift its head from its milk. To the rabbit, the cat as a natural enemy appears in the largeness of its physical strength and is a "monument of cat," but in the light of the moon—the light of the imagination—a change takes place. The rabbit, possessed with the sense of himself, loses his fear of the cat as his own imagination transports him into a world of his potentialities. And in this world the light is a "rabbit-light," since it is the rabbit's imagination that illuminates the scene. The rabbit becomes the center of his world, as men, when thinking about themselves, become the center of the universe. The imaginary world of the rabbit forms about him: "And east rushes west and west rushes down/ No matter," for there is "no matter" in the rabbit's world of imagination. The rabbit grows until he "fills the four corners of night," and the red cat is seen only in the "fur-light," the rabbit-light of imagination. And the stature of the rabbit increases "humped high, humped up" until he replaces the cat as the monument and becomes himself "a carving in space." In the final correspondence, the cat is as small and insignificant as "a bug in the grass"; it is a "green" cat, for the greater reality of the rabbit's imagination has dwarfed the limited reality of the cat.

Although we must always achieve a "oneness" with the place we inhabit, our correspondence to reality changes with our thinking and becomes more complex as the imagination discovers new possibilities of reality. In the poem "What We See Is What We Think" (p. 459) there is a less dramatic but more explicit statement of seen things changing to things thought:

At twelve, the disintegration of afternoon
Began, the return to phantomerei, if not
To phantoms. Till then, it had been the other way:

One imagined the violet trees but the trees stood green,
At twelve, as green as ever they would be.
The sky was blue beyond the vaultiest phrase.

Twelve meant as much as: the end of normal time,
Straight up, an élan without harrowing,
The imprescriptible zenith, free of harangue,

Twelve and the first gray second after, a kind
Of violet gray, a green violet, a thread
To weave a shadow's leg or sleeve, a scrawl

On the pedestal, an ambitious page dog-eared
At the upper right, a pyramid with one side
Like a spectral cut in its perception, a tilt

And its tawny caricature and tawny life,
Another thought, the paramount ado . . .
Since what we think is never what we see.

In this poem, day and the color green represent the reality of perception. As we pass the noon hour, the absolute hour, when things are "green as ever they would be" and "What we see is what we think," we are headed toward the night, the time of the moon and imagination with "the return to phantomerei, if not/ To phantoms." The mind turns with the symbolic turning of the day until images of the imagination form on the mind's bright screen: "a thread/ To weave a shadow's leg or sleeve, a scrawl/ On the pedestal, an ambitious page dog-eared," "a pyramid with one side/ Like a spectral cut in its perception, a tilt/ And its tawny caricature and tawny life . . ." Here in its full activity we see the "paramount ado" of human thought, and the mind has sailed beyond the orbit of perception so that "what we think is never what we see."

It would be incorrect, however, to think that for Stevens all poetry or all knowledge is a continuous rational process of extrospective and introspective observation. The irrational element in our sense of the world is part of our imagination, and has its own complex logic possessing a rationality of its own: "We shall return at twilight from the lecture/ Pleased that the irrational is rational" (p. 406). It is not enough to explain feeling by showing our relationships to the world. The immediacy of the world that we experience is always more profound than our knowledge of this immediacy.

The apparent dichotomy between things as they are known to the perceptual eye and things as they are known by human feeling and imagination is Stevens' greatest concern. Infinite reality does not prefer one or the other, but rather includes both. And if a satisfactory resolution is to be achieved, then these antinomies must be seen as aspects of one thing: for Stevens this thing is *change*. In a world without change it is possible to be completely rational. Devoid of happiness and unhappiness, the only feeling one could have is to know, and though this might be bliss for angels, it would not be bliss for men whose irrationality is often the source of their deepest feelings. In the cycle of abandonment and return to strict, perceptible reality the imagination, in its flight, has added itself to "things as they are."

FOUR

Reality, Imagination and the
Supreme Fiction

❃ Reality is the beginning not the end.

The paramount concern of the imagination is the relationship of things. It continues to seek out the order to which everything belongs and it expects of this order a cosmic harmony. Stevens' ideas about the imagination owe a debt to Coleridge, whose famous description of the imagination states that it

. . . reveals itself in the balance or reconcilement of opposite or discordant qualities: of sameness, with difference; of the general, with the concrete; the idea, with the image; the individual with the representative; the sense of novelty and freshness, with old and familiar objects; a more than usual state of emotion with more than usual order . . .

To achieve the unity of "opposite or discordant qualities," Stevens opens his intelligence to an unlimited world of possibility in which paradox, abstraction and illusion are parts of reality, which may be seen as static but which is always changing.

Stevens' reality is dependent on the imagination for realization; and the imagination, as part of a greater reality, is dependent upon itself for realization. But the imagination is also capable of denying its own elaborations of images in order to reach back into external reality and perceive "the plum," as Stevens says, that "survives its poems." In its self-consciousness, however, the imagination recognizes its own function: it discovers forms within the possibilities of reality among its own inventions. It moves from perception, expanding its vision of reality with the addition of its own forms, and then, as these forms cease to satisfy the human instinct for what is literally real, the imagination returns to perception and begins anew. Reality will appear different at every point of this cycle—the imagination moving from immediate perception and the imagination moving toward it. The evolving imagination sees reality symbolized by summer, when the earth proliferates its imagery. Reality, seen during this interval of the cycle, depends upon the imagination's discovery of resemblances and correspondences. The contracting imagination abandons all elaborations to return to the essential fact of the world, perceptible only to the perfect photographic eye, and is symbolized by winter when the earth strips itself of summer's images. Stevens constantly moves between these two views of reality. If we see that the source of reality is place, the world, and that the source of imagination is person, the poet, then we can understand why it is so important to Stevens to achieve the unity of person and place, for it is also the unity of imagination and reality.

In "Description without Place" (p. 339) Stevens tells us that we live in a world of appearances, of "seeming": "The sun is an example. What it seems/ It is and in such seeming all things are." It is impossible for us to identify things except in reference to their "seeming." These seemings, the result of perception becoming conception, are always different from "things as they are," so that we do not live in a world of "flat appearance." "It [seeming] is a sense/ To which we refer experience, a knowledge/ Incognito," and thus it includes our memory of the past and our anticipation of the future. It does not actually describe the object of its contemplation, and, therefore, Stevens calls it "description without place." It is sight plus self: "Description is/ Composed of a sight indifferent to the eye." It is the reconstruction of the world by the imagination:

It is an expectation, a desire,

. . . . .

A little different from reality:
The difference that we make in what we see

And our memorials of that difference . . .

Description, as seeming, is most significant as the dramatization of the unity of person and place: "Description is revelation. It is not/ The thing described." Reality and imagination, sun and moon, by the description of seeming, become in Stevens' poems the "book of reconciliation." Reality without imagination is mere fact; imagination without reality, mere fancy. Stevens continues to argue for their unity: "The imagination loses vitality as it ceases to adhere to what is real." And also, "The world about us would be desolate except for the world within us." Stevens distinguishes the reality of fact from

the reality of the imagination but insists on their unification, so that the life lived and the scene in which it is lived
may enrich each other.

Man is always dependent upon reality as fact, although
it is not his final reality, and he returns again and again
to fact for his imagination's fresh beginning. Since description, the seeming of art, is the means by which man
unifies his world, it is clear why Stevens feels that "The
theory of description matters most." As man comes more
to imitate the description of himself, he extends himself
into the realm where everything he knows becomes more
fully "alive with its own seemings, seeming to be/ Like
rubies reddened by rubies reddening."

Poetry is seeming, the imagination's greatest addition to
reality as fact. The central metaphor of "The Man on the
Dump" (p. 201) is that of a poet sitting amid a pile of his
own images which have become irrelevant to the world
of fact and are, therefore, no longer part of the correspondence of person and place: "Ho-ho . . . The dump
is full/ Of images." The whole poem is giddy with images
that have lost their relationship to reality, and which the
imagination must abandon. Step by step, in careful con-

tiguity, the imagination begins the return to a new reality; and "One feels the purifying change. One rejects/ The trash." But it is at the very moment when the imagination rejects the trash, "the janitor's poems/ Of every day," that the imagination starts on a new cycle and moves toward its "summer" flourishing, and then

> . . . the moon creeps up
> To the bubbling of bassoons. That's the time
> One looks at the elephant-colorings of tires.
> Everything is shed; and the moon comes up as the moon
> (All its images are in the dump) and you see
> As a man (not like an image of a man),
> You see the moon rise in the empty sky.

Images like the moon and musical instruments are indications that the elaborating imagination has come into play, and in this poem, with the purging of the remnants of an outworn reality, the imagination begins to freshen the world with new seeming. The moon of the imagination rises in an "empty sky," which, in its transparence, symbolizes the vision of new possibility: "Where was it one first heard the truth? The the" says Stevens, ending the poem, and before we can name the truth there will be new trash in the dump that must be cleared. The poet will have to begin again.

When one reaches the extreme, where all images are stripped away, one knows only winter reality and has a mind like that of "The Snow Man," who "beholds/ Nothing that is not there" because his mind has stripped itself of all imagination. At this point the poet must turn to the reality of fact as discovered by the coldest eye of perception, searching out resemblances and attempting the colligation of experience. From the winter within us is born the desire for poetry, for when we know that what we have will not suffice we feel desire's earliest stirrings, as in "Notes toward a Supreme Fiction" (p. 382):

And not to have is the beginning of desire.
To have what is not is its ancient cycle.
It is the desire at the end of winter, when

It observes the effortless weather turning blue
And sees the myosotis on its bush.
Being virile, it hears the calendar hymn.

It knows that what it has is what is not
And throws it away like a thing of another time,
As morning throws off stale moonlight and shabby sleep.

Although for Stevens winter symbolizes the time when the imagination is most still, it also represents the imagination's power of self-discipline which enables the poet to return to the root of knowledge, the material actuality of fact. With fact, we have nothing but our perceptual acuity and the desire to expand things as they are. It is at this phase of the cycle when we have discarded everything not immediately part of the scene, and are left with the scene's mere factuality, that we become aware of our need for the imagination. As easily as the planets wheel about the sun, winter takes on the color of the imagination, "the effortless weather turning blue," and fixes its sight upon an early image, "sees the myosotis on its bush." So the imagination "throws off stale moonlight," discards its old images, casts them into the "dump" of the obsolete, and is left in winter from which a new poetry for a new season must come to birth.

Although the imagination must always return—in the

cycle of change—to winter, Stevens is happiest with summer's arrival, for it is the time when the imagination flourishes. The title, *Transport to Summer* (the original book containing "Notes toward a Supreme Fiction" (p. 380), expresses the same idea as the title of the poem. In the last section of this long poem Stevens evokes a deeply personal image of a girl as a symbol of summer: "Fat girl, terrestrial, my summer, my night." *Transport to Summer* can be read in two ways: "transport" meaning travel or journey and "transport" meaning ecstasy or rapture. Stevens journeys toward summer in order to achieve the "Supreme Fiction," a fiction that results in deepest feeling and is the imagination's truth made real.

In summer we see things as we feel they are. Our sense of them is composed of the emotion they evoke in us as well as of their factual presence. It is this complex existence of objects that Stevens describes in "Bouquet of Roses in Sunlight" (p. 430):

Say that it is a crude effect, black reds,
Pink yellows, orange whites, too much as they are
To be anything else in the sunlight of the room,

Too much as they are to be changed by metaphor,
Too actual, things that in being real
Make any imaginings of them lesser things.

And yet this effect is a consequence of the way
We feel and, therefore, is not real, except
In our sense of it, our sense of the fertilest red,

Of yellow as first color and of white,
In which the sense lies still, as a man lies,
Enormous, in a completing of his truth.

Our sense of these things changes and they change,
Not as in metaphor, but in our sense
Of them. So sense exceeds all metaphor.

It exceeds the heavy changes of the light.
It is like a flow of meanings with no speech
And of as many meanings as of men.

We are two that use these roses as we are,
In seeing them. This is what makes them seem
So far beyond the rhetorician's touch.

Roses seen in sunlight appear so real in their vivid brightness that we hesitate to think this vividness is any quality
we supply in perceiving them, but assume rather it is a
luminescence the roses have of their own. They seem "too
actual," and yet, Stevens says, the brightness of their appearance "is a consequence of the way/ We feel." It is our
sense of things that is most vivid, and though the "seeming" that results from perception is alive with such intensity that it appears to be beyond metaphor, we realize
that metaphor provides the self-awareness of intense feeling. Thus imagination, the source of metaphor and of
seeming, is also the source of profoundest feeling: "the
sense lies still, as a man lies,/ Enormous, in a completing
of his truth." "The sense lies still" is the quiet eye that
takes in the world; and the senses also lie in that they
fabricate the world we know. But fabrication need not
only imply distortion, it may also mean building, for
through the poet's fabrication he becomes "Enormous, in
a completing of his truth." It is because our senses
are fabricators that the truths we come to hold must be
fictions. The fabricating impulse produces the imaginative
birth, the bounty of human values, purpose and meaning.

Stevens defines "sense" and "seeming" as metaphor, since they are our description of things in terms of the full response they evoke in us. As our sense of things changes, they change, and we know them in their new seeming. "So sense exceeds all metaphor," because it constantly changes and exists with us in present time, while a metaphor fixes an object in a given conception, removing it from time and change. Our sense of things is always "beyond the rhetorician's touch," because it is always with us, contained in the immediate present, changing.

Our sense of things (their seeming) is the product of the imagination, which creates a heightened reality from "things as they are" by illuminating with its own light a world that is otherwise dark with fact and devoid of feeling. This is the theme Stevens dramatizes in "Phosphor Reading by His Own Light" (p. 267):

It is difficult to read. The page is dark.
Yet he knows what it is that he expects.

The page is blank or a frame without a glass
Or a glass that is empty when he looks.

The greenness of night lies on the page and goes
Down deeply in the empty glass . . .

Look, realist, not knowing what you expect.
The green falls on you as you look,

Falls on and makes and gives, even a speech.
And you think that that is what you expect,

That elemental parent, the green night,
Teaching a fusky alphabet.

Phosphor is the imagination. Without his light the book of the world is dark and difficult to read. Phosphor knows what "he expects" because he can tell by his own light that he is part of what is real, and therefore he expects a world whose book will include him. But he has not yet been written into the book, "the page is blank," and only the world's reality, "the greenness of night," is on the page which, as an "empty glass," is still the potential mirror of mankind. Phosphor expects to discover himself on the empty page, while the realist, believing in only the world, cannot anticipate any writing in the book that will be about him. But the book contains the "greenness of night" which includes the realist, who then sees himself in the reflected light and is given the speech that is the gift of self-discovery. Speech and imagination are contained in the reality of the world, "that elemental parent," whose "alphabet" will, in time, describe us. From our awareness of the "greenness of night" we discover the language to express this awareness in which the real and the imagined are aspects of the same thing.

The light of the imagination helps us read the book of the world, but it is also an inner light that has a resourcefulness of its own, and brings to life things that without its illumination are desolate and drab. In "Disillusionment of Ten O'Clock" (p. 66) Stevens is commenting on modern man's lack of imaginative convictions:

The houses are haunted
By white night-gowns.
None are green,
Or purple with green rings,
Or green with yellow rings,
Or yellow with blue rings.

None of them are strange,
With socks of lace
And beaded ceintures.
People are not going
To dream of baboons and periwinkles.
Only, here and there, an old sailor,
Drunk and asleep in his boots,
Catches tigers
In red weather.

Stevens' titles often provide us with his attitude toward the action that takes place within a poem, and therefore they have a special function in the structure of the poem. If the title is humorous, ironic or ambiguous, it is necessary to regard the poem from this perspective. "Disillusionment of Ten O'Clock" contrasts people who "are not going/ To dream of baboons and periwinkles" with the old, drunk and dreaming sailor who "Catches tigers/ In red weather." The inability of these people to live in the colored world of the imagination, to be ghosts dressed in "purple with green rings," is their disillusionment. Stevens' irony is severe in its judgment; clearly he would not have the sailor abandon the illusion that enables him to catch tigers. And we may conjecture further: why are ghosts in "white night-gowns" any more real than ghosts attired in color? The color red suggests the intensity of the sailor's commitment to imagination, and if we believe with Stevens that the imagination is "The magnificent cause of being, the one reality/ In this imagined world," then surely the dreaming sailor's illusion saves us from the disillusionment which reduces modern life to a drab reality.

The "disillusionment" in this poem would deprive us of the fictions that enrich our lives. In "Notes toward a Supreme Fiction," Stevens presents to us the abstraction— a supreme fiction—which would totally disabuse us of our disillusionment and would fill reality with the ultimate fullness of imagination. Such a "fiction" can, of course, only be approached, not reached, and so Stevens' "Notes" move "toward" it. Stevens gives us the categories that reveal the nature of this fiction by dividing his poem into three sections: "It Must Be Abstract," "It Must Change," and "It Must Give Pleasure." The first section opens with Stevens addressing an "ephebe" (a youth just entering manhood) (pp. 380–381) and Stevens tells him

that he must return to the source of reality—fact, and must
see the sun in its own idea, not the ideas of his predecessor's imaginings,

> And see the sun again with an ignorant eye
> And see it clearly in the idea of it.
> . . . . .
> How clean the sun when seen in its idea,
> Washed in the remotest cleanliness of a heaven
> That has expelled us and our images . . .

Phoebus was one of many images of the sun in man's
endless attempt to know reality by describing it. But old
images must be continually rejected in the search for the
"Supreme Fiction," the infinite and complete reality,
which is always beyond our most brilliant descriptions:
"Phoebus is dead, ephebe. But Phoebus was/ A name for
something that never could be named."

The ephebe is told to perceive the idea of the "invented
world," since the idea of the "sun" (symbolizing the actual, not the invented world) is "inconceivable." What
Stevens means is that knowledge begins with what our

senses tell us, and from this we may then abstract an idea of the world which is an invention. And because this "idea of the sun" is inconceivable, we must struggle for knowledge within the limits of our ability to invent, for these inventions, our fictions, are also our truths. Stevens' first mandate is that we must always keep referring to the world that we can observe, and the return to winter is, symbolically, the turning to a new beginning in the necessary attempt to renew our fictions. One of the functions of poetry, then, is to approach the source of all our ideas, images and metaphors, so that the closer we come to the first idea the closer we come to the fountain-source of reality: "The poem refreshes life so that we share,/ For a moment, the first idea." But each poet knows that there was a poet before him to sing the description of each idea, that "The first idea was not our own." And from this the poet knows, too, that "There was a myth before the myth began,/ Venerable and articulate and complete./ From this the poem springs."

Stevens believes that myth embodies fundamental psychological truths, that the poet who understands the human predicament will approach the archetypal truth of myth in his art. Stevens' heroes, his giants, major men, men of crystal, are such poets. For them the process of composing consists of the discovery of the relationships, the balances in nature: "not balances/ That we achieve but balances that happen,/ As a man and woman meet and love forthwith." Since our myths are fictions, they must be abstractions of "the Truth," for they cannot be Truth itself if reality is infinite. They are the shadows on the cave, the imitations of the first idea (p. 388):

> The major abstraction is the idea of man
> And major man is its exponent, abler
> In the abstract than in his singular . . .

Man's major subject is himself. The hero is the abstraction that defines all men as the sum of their possibilities, for this is how the poet sees all men as one, and this one in all its collective largeness (p. 389):

> What rabbi, grown furious with human wish,
> What chieftain, walking by himself, crying
> Most miserable, most victorious,

Does not see these separate figures one by one,
And yet see only one, in his old coat,
His slouching pantaloons, beyond the town,

Looking for what was, where it used to be?
Cloudless the morning. It is he. The man
In that old coat, those sagging pantaloons,

It is of him, ephebe, to make, to confect
The final elegance, not to console
Nor sanctify, but plainly to propound.

The fiction toward which we strive must be an abstraction propounding what we might become and still remain human, and it is the imagination, Stevens holds, that provides us with the ability to fulfill these possibilities: "The imagination is the only genius. It is intrepid and eager and the extreme of its achievement lies in abstraction (*Nec. Ang.*, p. 139)." Our fictions must exceed actuality to embody the abstraction of collective man, and they must also be able to reject their abstractions when they have ceased to remember man as he actually is. This expansion and contraction is Stevens' description of the natural phenomena of change: the seasons turn, day becomes night, and the shore is changed by the removal of a single shell. Not only must fictions include the concept of change, but they must change themselves in order to be true to the world they would describe. This does not mean that Stevens concerns himself only with what is ephemeral, for the abstraction of a "supreme fiction" conceives of an original and complete idea of the world, and as we approach this supreme fiction through our mundane fictions we thus approach the knowledge of the eternal.

Although change takes place within a closed system— the world of reality—it has infinite possibilities, just as the numbers one and two comprise a closed system and yet contain an infinite number of fractions between them. Stevens includes in man as he is all the possibilities of man as he could be. This, too, is a closed system, for man can never become an angel, although he can become "major man" (p. 389):

. . . Thus the constant

Violets, doves, girls, bees and hyacinths
Are inconstant objects of inconstant cause
In a universe of inconstancy.

99

The "Violets, doves, girls, bees and hyacinths" are constant in our idea of them, as a memory is constant in the mind though the remembered object has long ago passed from sight. Fiction is memory made permanent with the clarity of perspective, so that we see things in our idea of them with a heightened vividness. Stevens often symbolizes the imagination and poetry by a musical instrument as "the clear viol of her memory" which suggests the inextricability of memory and imagination. Although the objects we find in the world "Are inconstant objects of inconstant cause/ In a universe of inconstancy," they can be constant in idea, memory and poetry.

The supreme fiction must be continually sought though it can never be reached, for it is infinite, and so we move through change, and when we say that something has happened we mean that it is different from what it was before because "nothing has happened" when "nothing has changed." The cause of major change is the merging of opposites: imagination and reality, person and place. The supreme fiction is the abstraction which, if realized, would express the final composition of all antinomies, and therefore it exists beyond change (p. 392):

100

Two things of opposite natures seem to depend
On one another, as a man depends
On a woman, day on night, the imagined

On the real. This is the origin of change.

Change is the process of becoming, and our sense of
change is part of the work of the imagination, which
manipulates the scenery and props on the stage of the
world, so that we, as actors, can always speak new roles
and sound those accents that make us appear to ourselves
as major man: "The freshness of transformation is/ The
freshness of a world. It is our own,/ It is ourselves, the
freshness of ourselves."

To take pleasure in something is to take it seriously,
whether it is comic or tragic. The pleasure we enjoy in
knowing a landscape, having an idea, or loving a woman
is our way of valuing them, and it is the measure of our
feeling that describes the qualities of things throughout
the world. Stevens believes that men primarily desire to
know, and therefore they name things in an attempt to
satisfy this desire. These names are fictions, for they are

not the things themselves. But Stevens is aware of the ultimate inability to fulfill the desire for complete knowledge, and he treasures the fleeting moments when we have glimpses into the truth of reality, when we write our poems. It has been said that without poetry people would never think of falling in love, and for Stevens the imagination is always the source and sustenance of love (p. 380):

And for what, except for you, do I feel love?
Do I press the extremest book of the wisest man
Close to me, hidden in me day and night?

And through the imagination we rise above mere animal instinct to higher feeling, to a love for the place in which we are, for imagination makes specific the bond by which a man and woman come together: "They married well because the marriage-place/ Was what they loved."

Facing the apparent antithesis of reality and the imagination, Stevens argues that they are part of each other, and, as they become more perfectly one in our sight, our world takes on its greatest order (p. 403):

102

He had to choose. But it was not a choice
Between excluding things. It was not a choice

Between, but of. He chose to include the things
That in each other are included, the whole,
The complicate, the amassing harmony.

This idea, central to his thought, is further expressed in
his essay, "The Noble Rider and the Sound of Words";
and for emphasis it is worth quoting here:

> . . . it [is] imperative for him to make a choice, to
> come to a decision regarding the imagination and reality;
> and he will find that it is not a choice of one over the other
> and not a decision that divides them, but something
> subtler, a recognition that here, too, as between these poles,
> the universal interdependence exists, and hence his choice
> and his decision must be that they are equal and insepara-
> ble. (*Nec. Ang.*, p. 24)

This is the spirit in which the uniting paradox is possible.
Only in this spirit can one conceive of the final order in
which the supreme fiction rests. The measure of our success in approaching the supreme fiction is in the pleasure

we receive from the orders we construct, for order, Stevens feels, is the apogee of man's delight.

In the ultimate order, everything partakes of everything else; there is no disunity, all becomes part of the One, the unifying whole that reconciles all opposites and brings all things together in felicitous relationship. Stevens expresses his faith in this order by continually turning back to earth to enjoy and to learn, for the devotion to learning is a way of life, a morality. The imagination brings man closer to reality by enabling him to create his fictions, his imitations of the actual order, out of the vast chaos of facts. The imagination "discovers order, but also imposes it." This distinction derives from Coleridge, who used the term "primary imagination" for the former and "secondary imagination" for the latter. But there is another activity of the mind which Coleridge calls "the fancy" and describes as "a mode of memory emancipated from the order of time and space." With Stevens, however, the fancy is not so clearly distinguished from the imagination, but is part of its functioning. Inasmuch as fancy is removed from "the order of time and space," that part of the imagination will produce fictions that do not describe what is real. The imagination, on the other hand, in its primary and secondary aspects, is the agency through which we most clearly understand the world, since in its workings it is able to form a finite image of infinite creation, or, in Coleridge's words, the imagination is "a repetition in the finite mind of the eternal act of creation in the infinite I AM."

Wallace Stevens' opening paragraph in his essay "The Noble Rider" contains a figure from Plato's dialogue, *The Phaedrus,* which describes the soul as "a pair of winged horses and a charioteer" seen traversing the heavens. Stevens describes it as "Plato's pure poetry" and augments his comment with Coleridge's phrase, "Plato's dear, gorgeous nonsense." Stevens says, in recounting the effect of Plato's passage:

The truth is that we have scarcely read the passage before we have identified ourselves with the charioteer, have, in fact, taken his place and, driving his winged horses, are traversing the whole heaven. Then suddenly we remember, it may be, that the soul no longer exists and we droop in our flight and at last settle on the solid ground. The figure becomes antiquated and rustic. (*Nec. Ang.,* pp. 3–4)

105

The figure has become "antiquated" because, in our time, it appeals only to the fancy. Stevens carried the concepts of fancy and imagination to their logical extreme:

> The imagination loses vitality as it ceases to adhere to what is real. When it adheres to the unreal . . . while its first effect may be extraordinary, that effect is the maximum effect that it will ever have . . . The case is, then, that we concede that the figure is all imagination. At the same time, we say that it has not the slightest meaning for us, except for its nobility. (*Nec. Ang.,* p. 6)

When Stevens says "the figure is all imagination," it is equivalent to Coleridge calling it fancy, for it is the imagination working apart from reality. Any image, metaphor or poem loses its vitality when the imagination that conceives it adheres to what is not real. And, conversely, a figure's vitality is assured when the imagination that produces it adheres to reality. A figure that comes from only the imagination is an invention, an imposition of order. A figure that comes from the union of imagination and reality is a discovery of order. Although for Stevens the fanciful, "all imagination," has its delight, nevertheless, it is the result of some abstract choice of the will that cannot survive, for if our fictions are to approach the truth they must be based on reality. In composing his fiction, Stevens postulates an absolute reality, and although the impositions of order by the fanciful imagination are "a brave affair" they will not suffice as fictions (pp. 403-404):

He imposes orders as he thinks of them,
As the fox and the snake do. It is a brave affair.

> . . . . .

> . . . But to impose is not
To discover. To discover an order as of
A season, to discover summer and know it,

To discover winter and know it well, to find,
Not to impose, not to have reasoned at all,
Out of nothing to have come on major weather,

It is possible, possible, possible. It must
Be possible. It must be that in time
The real will from its crude compoundings come,

Seeming, at first, a beast disgorged, unlike,
Warmed by a desperate milk. To find the real,
To be stripped of every fiction except one,

The fiction of an absolute—Angel,
Be silent in your luminous cloud and hear
The luminous melody of proper sound.

The invention of an order by the imagination will never lead to the discovery of a real order. This discovery cannot take place through reason, for that would be to impose our own logic, our own order upon the real as does the "logical lunatic." The real order is luminous with possibility like the angel in the "luminous cloud," and the "luminous melody" sings of this reality, for it is a music proper to mankind. The "angel" of reality will describe himself in a later poem as "the necessary angel of earth,/ Since, in my sight, you see the earth again," and become important enough to have Stevens' book of essays named in his honor.

In *The Necessary Angel* Stevens tells us that the imagination has no material existence but is an essence that is vividly present and is analogous only to light. Therefore, space, air, the depths of the sky, symbolize, for Stevens, the infinity of reality's possibilities into which the imagination can begin to see, and the sky is then like a mirror which reflects an image of the abstraction of collective man. But where does man end and his imaginings of himself begin? And how far can man extend himself through the vast aisles of space into "heaven"? "If the angel in his cloud,/ . . . Leaps downward through evening's revelations,/ . . . Am I that imagine this angel less satisfied?/ . . . Is it he or is it I that experience this?" To what extent does man become what he imagines himself to be? Is to know the angel in our imagination also to share his joy and to sit beside him on his cloud? Are the limits of our experience only those of our imagination, so that if it assumes the guise of an angel we will share his existence (pp. 404–405).

Is it I then that keep saying there is an hour
Filled with expressible bliss, in which I have

No need, am happy, forget need's golden hand,
Am satisfied without solacing majesty,
And if there is an hour there is a day,

There is a month, a year, there is a time
In which majesty is a mirror of the self:
I have not but I am and as I am, I am.

These external regions, what do we fill them with
Except reflections, the escapades of death,
Cinderella fulfilling herself beneath the roof?

We are not in need of "solacing majesty," for we will find
the majesty that lies within us "that is a mirror of the
self," and though Cinderella's roof suggests the borders
of her limitation, yet within the walls of her life she will
fulfill herself.

Man may have the stuff of angels within him, but he is
not an angel; he is of earth and enjoys the pleasures of
earth. In the last two parts of this poem Stevens sings of
the endless round of earth's richness and pleasure, and
invokes the birds, the spontaneous poets of nature, to
sing with him (pp. 405–406):

Whistle aloud, too weedy wren. I can
Do all that angels can. I enjoy like them,
Like men besides, like men in light secluded,

Enjoying angels. Whistle, forced bugler,
That bugles for the mate, nearby the nest,
Cock bugler, whistle and bugle and stop just short,

Red robin, stop in your preludes, practicing
Mere repetitions. These things at least comprise
An occupation, an exercise, a work,

A thing final in itself and, therefore, good:
One of the vast repetitions final in
Themselves and, therefore, good, the going round

And round and round, the merely going round,
Until merely going round is a final good,
The way wine comes at a table in a wood.

And we enjoy like men, the way a leaf
Above the table spins its constant spin,
So that we look at it with pleasure, look

At it spinning its eccentric measure. Perhaps,
The man-hero is not the exceptional monster,
But he that of repetition is most master.

Man enjoys existence both as angel and as man, and, by
performing in song like the bird, man shares in the eternal
repetition of the original creative act. Each repetition is a
finite aspect of the infinite phenomenon of creation, so

that each repetition is an act of affirmation and of faith. Repetition as metaphor, poem or song is part of the infinite change that returns us to the core of life, and as such is an attempt to know reality by imitatively re-creating it. Stevens says that the hero must be the master of repetition, and therefore he will be the poet of reality.

Describing the "fat girl," his symbol for the flowering of the world in the imaginative mind, Stevens portrays her as sensual and elusive, various beyond our best metaphor or poem, part of all change, and never finally known (pp. 406–407):

Fat girl, terrestrial, my summer, my night,
How is it I find you in difference, see you there
In a moving contour, a change not quite completed?

You are familiar yet an aberration.
Civil, madam, I am, but underneath
A tree, this unprovoked sensation requires

That I should name you flatly, waste no words,
Check your evasions, hold you to yourself.
Even so when I think of you as strong or tired,

Bent over work, anxious, content, alone,
You remain the more than natural figure. You
Become the soft-footed phantom, the irrational

Distortion, however fragrant, however dear.
That's it: the more than rational distortion,
The fiction that results from feeling. Yes, that.

They will get it straight one day at the Sorbonne.
We shall return at twilight from the lecture
Pleased that the irrational is rational,

Until flicked by feeling, in a gildered street,
I call you by name, my green, my fluent mundo.
You will have stopped revolving except in crystal.

The "unprovoked sensation," man's spontaneous desire to
know and therefore to name, would have her held to one
thing, one aspect. But this cannot be done; she will change
and proliferate the feeling we have for her. The name we
give her exists only in the present moment as "the fiction
that results from feeling." Only by an abstraction—the
supreme fiction—can we imagine her in infinity; this ab-

straction is symbolized here by a crystal, the perfect glass that reflects everything.

The epilogue of the poem is spoken directly to the reader as if he were a soldier, fighting Blake's "mental strife" on the battlefields of the mind (p. 407):

Soldier, there is a war between the mind
And sky, between thought and day and night. It is
For that the poet is always in the sun,

Patches the moon together in his room
To his Virgilian cadences, up down,
Up down. It is a war that never ends.

This is our war as well as the poet's; it can never be finally won, but must be continually fought. For this we must stand in the light of reality, "the sun," and must stand in the light of our own imagination, patching "the moon together," until the real and the imaginary are one, until sun and moon are seen as part of a single order. "How simply the fictive hero becomes the real," Stevens says, "How gladly with proper words the soldier dies,/ If he must, or lives on the bread of faithful speech." The proper words are those that describe us as we are. To die with these words is to know death as part of the reality to which we belong, and to accept it. And Stevens places his faith in the felicity of this reality, in this absolute that endlessly inspires our fictions, and therefore his appropriate ritual is that of "faithful speech." In this poem Stevens' imagination makes the choice of earth as the proper place for man, and it is of this choice that Stevens writes in *The Necessary Angel:* "The great poems of heaven and hell have been written and the great poem of the earth remains to be written."

The imagination is not identical with the Self; it has its wings, a freedom that enables it to soar beyond the Self and to see the world with an eye unbiased by any personal animus or eccentricity, and even to see the Self with this same unbiased vision. To write about one's own imagination is not to write autobiography. And in this we can account for the difference between the comic mode of Stevens and the tragic mode of Yeats. Yeats' subject is himself, and his greatness lies in the body of his work which discloses with excruciating honesty the development of a man from youth, through maturity, to age. We come to feel that his history is something more than he himself was at any given moment, that his history is itself a parable. Yeats feels all life converging upon him; he sees its meaning in his own struggles, disappointments and reconciliations. He is the center of the universe, life triumphs or fails in his joys and sorrows and through the action of his works and his intelligence. Stevens, on the other hand, does not take himself as his subject, but rather takes the imagination or the world. He writes about what is immortal—mankind—not about what is mortal—himself; he writes about the drama of reality, not the drama of personality. Yeats' subject is finite, it shows an arc of development; Stevens' subject is infinite, it describes a circle. For this reason, Stevens' personal development is not important as is Yeats', because Stevens' subject is inexhaustible and his triumph is that he never becomes exhausted by it. From his earliest to his very last poems written when he was in his seventies, his imagination never ceased to surprise him, to delight him, and to make new discoveries for him. In one of his last poems, "Note on Moonlight" (p. 531), we see him affirming a world

that is animated by imagination, "Is active with a power,
an inherent life," so that he still can feel the universe opening up to him in the greenest of beginnings:

The one moonlight, the various universe, intended
So much just to be seen—a purpose, empty
Perhaps, absurd perhaps, but at least a purpose,
Certain and ever more fresh. Ah! Certain, for sure . . .

FIVE

Nothingness, Chaos and Order

In things seen and unseen, created from nothingness,
The heavens, the hells, the worlds, the longed-for lands.

"Nothingness" in Stevens' vocabulary represents the reality one would see with the perfect perceptual eye devoid of all imagination. It is the reality of the world stripped of all its "seeming." It is the poverty suggested by winter when everything is reduced to its minimum, when the tree stands before us in its nakedness merely as fact, and we have forgotten the leaves it once bore and will flourish again in the summer winds. To understand the abstraction of "nothingness" is to have the earliest vision of reality, for "nothingness," like winter, is a beginning.

It is this beginning that will lead to the summer imagination by which reality will be known in its fullness. And it is this movement from winter to summer that postulates as its culmination the "supreme fiction," which is the ultimate description of reality. "Nothingness" and the "supreme fiction" are polarities that are never reached, but within which we move through a cyclical change, like the cycle of the seasons. These abstractions are themselves conceptions of the mind and, as such, are part of the total reality that includes the imaginary as well as the material. Stevens says the poet "must be able to abstract himself and also to abstract reality, which he does by placing it in his imagination" (*Nec. Ang.,* p. 23). The abstraction of a "supreme fiction," then, describes reality as the relationship of facts and our correspondence to them; while the abstraction of "nothingness" describes reality as isolated fact, fact unchanged by our perception of it. This explains why Stevens says the "opposite of 'fiction' is not 'truth' but 'fact,' " and in his essay "The Figure of the Youth as a Virile Poet," he says:

We have excluded absolute fact as an element of poetic truth. But this has been done arbitrarily and with a sense of absolute fact as fact destitute of any imaginative aspect whatever. Unhappily the more destitute it becomes the more it begins to be precious. (*Nec. Ang.,* p. 60)

The simple reason for fact's preciousness is that it is the beginning, like winter, summer's predecessor and parent; it is the source to which the imagination must refer, the brick with which it must build.

The symbols that Stevens uses to describe the abstraction of "nothingness" are: glass, air, ice, light, and winter-cold. The quality these images share is an apparent sparsity of physical presence. They are translucent and conducive to sight, and then to a fresh vision into the possibility of things.

These images seem closely related to those used by Mallarmé when describing his ideal state of contemplation. This state, the realm of poetry, resembles death and nothingness to Mallarmé, and so nothingness represents for him a removal from reality, while for Stevens it represents an approach, not a realm where contemplation exists as an end for its own satisfaction.

"The Snow Man" is the first of the early poems to describe a winter-cold scene in connection with "nothingness." In this poem, life is seen at its barest, the point at which there is "nothing" left but minimum, factual reality. In "Cortège for Rosenbloom" (p. 79) Stevens is dramatizing the idea of death as "nothingness," as absolute fact, before we come to see its relationship to life as we do in "Sunday Morning" where, quite differently, it is the "mother of beauty." The repeated rhyme of "dead" and "tread" effects a heavy emphasis on the word "dead." The scene is a "region of frost"; the "chirr of gongs" and "chitter of cries" are sounds suggestive of cold, and the "infants of nothingness" are among the carriers taking Rosenbloom to his grave "in a place in the sky." Life is at its lowest ebb as in the season of winter, and the irony in the name "Rosenbloom" in this poem is the irony of death. Metaphorically, the "infants of nothingness" carry us to the reality of this death.

In "Of Heaven Considered as a Tomb" (p. 56) we find a body of imagery closely related to that of "Cortège for Rosenbloom." Death is associated with the sky; again the season is winter:

What word have you, interpreters, of men
Who in the tomb of heaven walk by night,
The darkened ghosts of our old comedy?

Do they believe they range the gusty cold,
With lanterns borne aloft to light the way,
Freemen of death, about and still about
To find whatever it is they seek? Or does
That burial, pillared up each day as porte
And spiritous passage into nothingness,
Foretell each night the one abysmal night,
When the host shall no more wander, nor the light
Of the steadfast lanters creep across the dark?
Make hue among the dark comedians,
Halloo them in the topmost distances
For answer from their icy Élysée.

Stevens' invocation to the "interpreters" to find out something about the dead where they dwell in "nothingness"
constitutes the first three lines and the last three. However, the poet's tone becomes satirical at the end. The dead
have left our "old comedy" and have become "dark
comedians." Is this darkness part of the night in which
they walk, and also part of the poverty of "nothingness"?
Two questions are asked in the poem. The first question
asks how the dead, "the darkened ghosts," regard themselves: "Do they believe they range the gusty cold,/ With

lanterns borne aloft to light the way,/Freemen of death, about and still about/ To find whatever it is they seek?" The second question is really Stevens' tentative answer: "Or does/ That burial, pillared up each day as porte/ And spiritous passage into nothingness,/ Foretell each night the one abysmal night,/ When the host shall no more wander, nor the light/ Of the steadfast lanterns creep across the dark?" Perhaps the "spiritous passage into nothingness" leads us beyond change, where seeking is no longer necessary, where reality exists as an absolute, and there is one night, "abysmal," for there is no time. Imaginatively, we follow the progress of these men's lanterns in heaven's tomb until their lanterns cease to "creep across the dark," and we can follow no longer. So the poet ironically tells the "interpreters" to call for an answer that they are unable to obtain.

Nothingness is a vision of reality seen—like death in the above poems—with a clear starkness, after the old outworn "seemings" of the imagination have been rejected. It is a vision like the clearness of night that enables us to see the moon in its isolation, or as in winter when everything is shrunken to its essential self, when you yourself are merely "the final dwarf of you./ That is woven and woven and waiting to be worn,/ Neither as mask nor as garment but as a being,/ Torn from insipid summer, for the mirror of cold" ("The Dwarf," p. 208). The earth in winter mirrors a contraction that takes place cyclically within the imagination. That which remains in the moment of deepest winter is what we are at the core, the dwarf of our summer self: We have been stripped of the correspondences that tied us to the rest of reality in summer (which now seems "insipid"). Analogically, as spring blooms, the dwarf will begin to grow until he once more becomes the "giant" of summer's zenith, when his imagination is at its fullest and fact is seen as a unit in an architecture of facts. But the cycle must complete itself, and so fruit begins to rot beneath the trees, the odor rises and dissipates, autumn passes, summer's images have been rejected, and thus we return to the "dwarf" of ourself for the new beginning. We can see then why summer is Stevens' favorite season, for it is the time when "what is possible/ Replaces what is not," when the imagination is most creatively at work.

In the cycle of the imagination moving from its latest

attempt to achieve the "supreme fiction" back to "noth-ingness," reality's source, there is the possibility of infinite change. The process of change is a dialectic of fictions in contention as descriptions of reality. At the moment when one idea, one fiction, has been rejected, and before a new fiction, a new idea, has been conceived, we are in what Stevens calls "chaos." Chaos is part of the principle of change. In "Extracts from Addresses to the Academy of Fine Ideas" (p. 252) he tells us that "The law of chaos is the law of ideas,/ Of improvisations and seasons of be-lief." Chaos is the law of life as flux, so that each idea, set in the atmosphere of its own particular season, is neces-sarily the imperfect image of the final "pure idea":

Ideas are men. The mass of meaning and
The mass of men are one. Chaos is not

The mass of meaning. It is three or four
Ideas or, say, five men or, possibly, six.

In the end, these philosophic assassins pull
Revolvers and shoot each other. One remains.

The mass of meaning becomes composed again.
He that remains plays on an instrument

A good agreement between himself and night,
A chord between the mass of men and himself,

Far, far beyond the putative canzones
Of love and summer. The assassin sings

In chaos and his song is a consolation.
It is the music of the mass of meaning.

And yet it is a singular romance,
This warmth in the blood-world for the pure idea,

This inability to find a sound,
That clings to the mind like that right sound, that song

Of the assassin that remains and sings
In the high imagination, triumphantly.

In a season the assassin of that season prevails and sings
of the "mass of meaning," but "his song is a consolation,"
it is not a final resolution. His song "is a singular ro-

mance," for he is a single assassin and not "the mass of men." The motive for his song is "This warmth in the blood-world for the pure idea," it is his tie to the "mass of meaning" and to the "mass of men." This song, when it approaches the "supreme fiction," "clings to the mind like the right sound" and "sings/ In the high imagination, triumphantly." But the imagination can only compose the "mass of meaning" theoretically in an absolute season of no change, so that we are always to some extent in chaos. Chaos is indigenous to any movement toward order. It is an endless number of assassins in seasonal groupings; it is an endless war in which one idea triumphs but for a season, for it is never the "pure idea."

The thesis of "Connoisseur of Chaos" (p. 215) is that both order and disorder are part of the process of change: "A. A violent order is disorder; and/ B. A great disorder is an order. These/ Two things are one." A. represents the disorder of the tyranny of one idea over another, and B. represents the ideal of order implicit in the consciousness of disorder. If there were in the world only disorder, no order could possibly come of it. If only one order existed, there could be no disorder, and therefore change and

chaos are dependent on both order and disorder. An order
then is a "seasonal" idea:

A. Well, an old order is a violent one.
This proves nothing. Just one more truth, one more
Element in the immense disorder of truths.
B. It is April as I write. The wind
Is blowing after days of constant rain.
All this, of course, will come to summer soon.

The blowing wind and rain is a disorder, and yet it will
come to be the order of summer in the proper course of
change. This idea of order becoming disorder and disorder becoming order is Stevens' definition of the world
in which we live. We move through seasons of truth.
What was, what is, and what will be, are not the Truth,
they are truths that are part of the Truth. They elude us,
and we piece together what we can, for our home is chaos
in which the "pensive man . . . sees that eagle float/ For
which the intricate Alps are a single nest."
To be in chaos is to know a particular without knowing
its relation to the universal, to be ignorant of the truth that

things exist together in relationship as they do for the man who, filled with desire, recognizes the object of his desire. This is his correspondence to the world, in which both he and the object are particulars in the whole of an embracing reality. An example of a man in chaos, on the other hand, from "Chaos in Motion and Not in Motion" (p. 357) is Ludwig Richter, who "Has lost the whole in which he was contained,/ Knows desire without an object of desire,/ All mind and violence and nothing felt." Chaos is the time when "summer is changed to winter," when old relations fall apart, when Ludwig Richter "knows he has nothing more to think about,/ Like the wind that lashes everything at once." Soon he may know the "nothingness" that finally comes with winter, when the wind stops and everything is cleared away: "One feels the purifying change. One rejects/ The trash." Then the imagination is ready to begin the reconstruction of a world.

"Nothingness" describes a world reduced to fact when fact is a particular isolated from the general. In one sense Stevens treasures this fact, and in another he finds it completely meaningless. He treasures it as a unit of reality, as a basis for something which is to be constructed by the imagination, and yet it is meaningless while still regarded as absolute fact. In "The Course of a Particular" (*Opus Post.*, p. 96) Stevens traces the particular to the point at which it becomes absolute fact, and exists only in relation to itself:

Today the leaves cry, hanging on branches swept by wind,
Yet the nothingness of winter becomes a little less.
It is still full of icy shades and shapen snow.

The leaves cry . . . One holds off and merely hears the cry.
It is a busy cry, concerning someone else.
And though one says that one is part of everything,

There is a conflict, there is a resistance involved;
And being part is an exertion that declines:
One feels the life of that which gives life as it is.

The leaves cry. It is not a cry of divine attention,
Nor the smoke-drift of puffed-out heroes, nor human cry.
It is the cry of leaves that do not transcend themselves,

In the absence of fantasia, without meaning more
Than they are in the final finding of the air, in the thing
Itself, until, at last, the cry concerns no one at all.

It is at the point of deepest "nothingness," when the world is reduced to fact, that the imagination begins again to piece together the whole. The change of seasons is a change in order as the facts are more or less composed and the whole more or less apparent. The difference between winter and summer is a difference in visible order, and it can be said, speaking symbolically, that the longing for winter is a desire for fact and the longing for summer is the desire for the relationships into which fact may enter. Ultimately, however, the imagination's desire for fact is inseparable from its wish to explore the possibilities of construction.

"Dezembrum" (p. 218) is about the contention between winter-desire and summer-desire. The title itself suggests a merging or confusion of differing things: perhaps it is a summer pronunciation of the month December in which the poem takes place:

I

Tonight there are only the winter stars.
The sky is no longer a junk-shop,

Full of javelins and old fire-balls,
Triangles and the names of girls.

II

Over and over again you have said,
This great world, it divides itself in two,
One part is man, the other god:
Imagined man, the monkish mask, the face.

III

Tonight the stars are like a crowd of faces
Moving round the sky and singing
And laughing, a crowd of men,
Whose singing is a mode of laughter,

IV

Never angels, nothing of the dead,
Faces to people night's brilliancy,
Laughing and singing and being happy,
Filling the imagination's need.

V

In this rigid room, an intenser love,
Not toys, not thing-a-ma-jigs—

The reason can give nothing at all
Like the response to desire.

We remember from "The Man on the Dump" the image of a man sitting amid a pile of discarded summer images. In "Dezembrum" one stage later in the cycle, we see that in December the rejection of images has cleared the "junk-shop" of the sky. One looks up and "there are only the winter stars," and thus winter-desire is satisfied, for "The sky is no longer a junk-shop,/ Full of javelins and old fire-balls,/ Triangles and the names of girls." In stanza II the poem's protagonist addresses himself to his lover, and recounts her statement of the division between winter-desire and summer-desire, in which the latter is associated with the elaborating imagination, "the monkish mask, the face." In stanza III, even in the depth of winter, the first stirrings of summer-desire are felt, and the stars must be seen as more than "only the winter stars," they must become stars that "are like a crowd of faces/ Moving round the sky and singing." Seeing them in this way, Stevens then tells us they are "filling the imagination's need." But it is a time of winter, and winter-desire calls with the loudest voice, demanding its need be satisfied: "In this rigid room" (the room of winter), "an intenser love" (winter-desire), not for things of the imagination, "not toys, not thing-a-ma-jigs." The desire for love is here immediate and stripped to its clearest delineation like the "winter stars." It presents itself in this clarity and demands first response ("The reason can give nothing at all/ Like the response to desire") and then in a later season the imagination's "faces to people night's brilliancy."

Winter-desire, however, always takes on new ambition, for the limited reality that it discovers is one of poverty. It is when one achieves the consciousness of "nothingness" that the imagination begins to explore the possibilities which will satisfy its summer-desire for an earthly paradise. Contained within the heart of winter-desire there lies the energy of summer-desire (p. 320):

. . . How cold the vacancy
When the phantoms are gone and the shaken realist
First sees reality. The mortal no
Has its emptiness and tragic expirations.
The tragedy, however, may have begun,

Again, in the imagination's new beginning,
In the yes of the realist spoken because he must
Say yes, spoken because under every no
Lay a passion for yes that had never been broken.

We might substitute the phrase "a passion for no" for winter-desire when it is still moving toward "nothingness," and the phrase "a passion for yes" for summer-desire. The rejection of the phantoms by the "mortal no" clears the stage of human life and leaves an emptiness, a "nothingness," which must be filled again by the imagination. This "nothingness" opens the possibility for all things which the imagination in time will attempt to supply, consumed with the "passion for yes" (pp. 320–321):

Panic in the face of the moon—round effendi
Or the phosphored sleep in which he walks abroad
Or the majolica dish heaped up with phosphored fruit
That he sends ahead, out of the goodness of his heart,
To anyone that comes—panic, because
The moon is no longer these nor anything
And nothing is left but comic ugliness

Or a lustred nothingness. Effendi, he
That has lost the folly of the moon because
The prince of the proverbs of pure poverty.
To lose sensibility, to see what one sees,
As if sight had not its own miraculous thrift,
To hear only what one hears, one meaning alone,
As if the paradise of meaning ceased
To be paradise, it is this to be destitute.
This is the sky divested of its fountains.

The moon, symbol of the imagination, is devoid of its
images; the phantoms have fled, and "nothing is left but
. . . a lustred nothingness." This luster is the brightness
by which one may see the possibility of things and anticipate their fulfillment. The "folly of the moon" is necessary, for it is part of our sensibility. Our senses, Stevens
says, which reveal the "seeming" of reality, have their
"own miraculous thrift," so that the change from coldest
winter to the height of summer is not a change from spirit
to body but from spirit to embodied spirit. The summer
world is filled with objects able to satisfy the imagination's
fullest desire, and one no longer must contemplate

winter's empty table, for the earth can satisfy man's profoundest need with a "paradise of meaning."

Reality, seen as "nothingness," is the abstraction of external fact devoid of seeming, so that Stevens says ironically in "Flyer's Fall" (p. 336) that in the "nothingness of human after-death,/ . . . We believe without belief, beyond belief." "Nothingness," then, is reality before the human element has entered in: "The nothingness was a nakedness, a point,/ Beyond which fact could not progress as fact." To progress beyond fact is to enter into seeming and poetry. In "Questions Are Remarks" (p. 462), where a little boy points to an object and asks, "Mother, what is that," Stevens says: "His question is complete because it contains/ His utmost statement. . . . As far as nothingness permits." The boy's question is his remark, as the title tells us, because it implies the simple factual belief in the existence of the object. His question has the freshness of "what?" not the tiredness of "why?" "He does not say, 'Mother, my mother, who are you,'/ The way the drowsy, infant, old men do."

Stevens' beginning is never arbitrary, just as winter is not, for his abstraction of "nothingness" is a stroke of clairvoyance as in "An Ordinary Evening in New Haven," where the very barrenness of winter becomes the source of a new vision (pp. 487–488):

The last leaf that is going to fall has fallen.
. . . . .
The wind has blown the silence of summer away.
. . . . .
The barrenness that appears is an exposing.
It is not part of what is absent, a halt
For farewells, a sad hanging on for remembrances.

It is a coming on and a coming forth.
. . . . .
The glass of the air becomes an element—
It was something imagined that has been washed away.
A clearness has returned. It stands restored.

It is not an empty clearness, a bottomless sight.
It is a visibility of thought,
In which hundreds of eyes, in one mind, see at once.

The imagination, now washed clear, is ready for a new "coming on and a coming forth," and this return to winter corresponds to the renewed search for a definition of reality: "To re-create, to use/ The cold and earliness and bright origin/ Is to search." The "inhalations of original cold and of original earliness" mark the awakening of the imagination, which then begins its inquiry into the "possibleness" of reality. Thus Stevens finds a symbol for "nothingness" in "the evening star,/ . . . That it is wholly an inner light, that it shines/ From the sleepy bosom of the real, re-creates,/ Searches a possible for its possibleness."

"Nothingness" includes as possibility all things seen or unseen which evade even a poet's most acute metaphor, as life itself evades any final description. And yet the poet emerges from the chaos of unidentified, unknown things, from the chaos of unrelated facts, having discovered that which already exists within "possibleness." The "central poem" is Stevens' phrase for the abstraction of the sum of all poetry that would describe the whole of reality. But "We do not prove the existence of the poem./ It is something seen and known in lesser poems," Stevens tells us in "A Primitive Like an Orb" (p. 440). The central poem is composed of an infinite number of smaller poems, and therefore it can be conceived of only in abstraction by "the lover, the believer and the poet" whose "words are chosen out of their desire,/ The joy of language, when it is themselves./ With these they celebrate the central poem,/ The fulfillment of fulfillments." As the central poem is an abstraction denoting the idea of the infinite expression of an infinite reality, so the "hero," the "giant," is an abstraction denoting the poet who composes the central poem (p. 443):

Here, then, is an abstraction given head,
A giant on the horizon, given arms,
A massive body and long legs, stretched out,
A definition with an illustration, not
Too exactly labelled, a large among the smalls
Of it, a close, parental magnitude,
At the centre on the horizon, concentrum, grave
And prodigious person, patron of origins.

For the giant the only limits are those of reality and of the imagination. He encompasses all individuals, all past, present and future; he exists in change, including all possibility. He is the "giant of nothingness" (p. 443):

143

That's it. The lover writes, the believer hears,
The poet mumbles and the painter sees,
Each one, his fated eccentricity,
As a part, but part, but tenacious particle,
Of the skeleton of the ether, the total
Of letters, prophecies, perceptions, clods
Of color, the giant of nothingness, each one
And the giant ever changing, living in change.

SIX

The Hero as the Final
Abstraction of Character

The central man, the human globe, responsive
As a mirror with a voice, the man of glass,
Who in a million diamonds sums us up.

Stevens' hero is not a man among us, but a man beyond us. He does not exist in our world except as abstraction. But, conscious of the idea of the hero, men labor to achieve nobility in the quotidian world, and it is the poet's work to make this idea vivid, since "The way through the world/ Is more difficult to find than the way beyond it" ("Reply to Papini," p. 446).

The hero is a man who has an eye for order, a "ten-foot poet among inchlings." He is the composite image of us all, a central figure, "Who in a million diamonds sums us up." The hero exists in our fictions, and Stevens says that the myth for our time in which the hero lives must be an ideal which becomes "blooded" as our belief in it grows and as we act according to its wisdom. The myth that enfolds the hero is made out of the appearances of things, which Stevens gives the elaborate dress of rhetoric and dazzling vocabulary. These objects of sight are important in themselves, for they comprise a world for the comedian who is in love with life because he can say delightful things about it, and who loves language for its own sake. It is the right world for Crispin, "The Comedian as the Letter C," who would agree with Stevens that "Life consists/ Of propositions about life." The comedian, the poet, the hero, are all makers of propositions about life, and in turn are propositions themselves when Stevens defines them.

Stevens assumes that the individual in the modern world is too small to shake the bracing pillars of society, and therefore he cannot be tragic. Certainly, we will not feel compassion or awe for Stevens' hero, for he does not live within a human situation as we ordinarily recognize it. He is a proposition, an abstraction, and therein lies his universal appeal. As "nothingness" is an expression for the infinite possibility of reality, so the hero is an expression for the infinite possibility of man. The hero, then, will be the poet who composes the central poem, and he will also be its subject. As idea, the hero is a fitting subject for

Stevens, who then attempts to reveal the correspondences between the idea of the hero and the feelings in us that are associated with it. In "Large Red Man Reading" (p. 423), for example, ghosts who "had expected more" returned to life to hear the large red man read "from the poem of life," and in reading from the "great blue tabulae" all objects "Took on color, took on shape and the size of things as they are/ And spoke the feeling for them, which was what they had lacked." No object, no idea, can be really known, Stevens believes, until its corresponding feelings also are known, and therefore to describe the idea of the hero, Stevens must find a way to communicate the emotion that is part of this idea.

As early as *Harmonium,* Stevens makes the association of poet and giant in "Bantams in Pine-Woods" (p. 75), where the "ten-foot poet" is seen through the eyes of the "inchlings" around him. This idea of the poet's largeness and his centrality in human affairs is developed in "Life on a Battleship" (*Opus Post.,* p. 77), where the captain of the ship proposes that he will organize the world by building one great ship: "Given what I intend,/ The ship would become the center of the world./ My cabin as the center of the ship and I/ As the center of the cabin." The captain, of course, is speculating about himself in the image of the hero, the "central man," and then he states dryly: "And once the thing was done, . . . the sorrow of the world, except/ As man is natural, would be at an end." The force of these lines must be due to the understatement of their idea, for they ironically express the impossibility of natural man's becoming the central man. Nevertheless, having conceived of the central man, the hero, man is changed as he thinks and acts in reference to this idealized image of himself. And it is this idealization that is the work of the poet's imagination, which Stevens says "is the power of the mind over the possibility of things" (*Nec. Ang.,* p. 136).

An ideal can absorb the endless attention of men because it is shiningly unattainable. For Stevens, the hero stands as the definition of such an ideal, so that he says in "Asides on the Oboe" (p. 250):

>   . . . [if] man is not enough,
> Can never stand as god, is ever wrong

150

In the end, however naked, tall, there is still
The impossible possible philosophers' man,
The man who has had the time to think enough . . .

The "impossible possible philosophers' man" is globe,
mirror, glass, diamond: as center, he reflects everything
in the world about him. Transparence is the quality of all
the images describing him, and we come to think of him
as a visibility through which we see the essential reality of
ourselves in all our inherent largeness. His poems are of a
world we desire to know and possess, and our poetry is
the means by which we attempt to fulfill this desire. "He
is the transparence of the place in which/ He is and in his
poems we find peace." It is necessarily the poet, therefore,
who is hero and leader because "he creates the world to
which we turn incessantly and without knowing it and
that he gives to life the supreme fictions without which
we are unable to conceive of it" (*Nec. Ang.*, p. 31). We
try constantly to extend our imaginations, to become one
with the central man; with him we suffer and with him
we find the "central evil" and the "central good." His
function as poet is to make "his imagination become the

light in the minds of others" (*Nec. Ang.,* p. 29) until we know "The glass man, without external reference."

Stevens describes our attempt to become one with the central man by saying that we move from a knowledge of fact as it first appears to a knowledge of fact as we prefer it. Since poetry is part of the structure of reality, the imagination adds to reality, reorganizing its facts, by inventing such fictions as the hero. The consciousness of the ideal of the hero, and the awareness of our inner cry to make the hero real, change fact until it becomes part of the "fictions" which give our lives the meaning and nobility we require they have. "Fact as we want it to be" is a description of fact as worthy of belief, as Stevens' belief in the hero is in man as he may come to be when acting out the possibilities that he has always possessed.

There is an irresistible need in man's nature to believe deeply in something beyond himself, and Stevens feels that in our age, as he says in "Examination of the Hero in a Time of War" (p. 273): "Unless we believe in the hero, what is there/ To believe?" Stevens' poems about the hero, therefore, are the rituals of his belief that fictions represent something grounded in reality. It is this

reality, composed of fact and imagination, that includes
the central man whom the poet must continue to seek:

Devise, devise, and make him of winter's
Iciest core, a north star, central
In our oblivion, of summer's
Imagination, the golden rescue . . .

In Stevens' season symbolism, winter is the time of isolated fact and summer is the time of the flourishing of the
imagination when fact becomes part of a structure of facts.
Viewed within this context, the above quotation becomes
rich: the hero, born in coldest winter, grows out of fact
"central/ In our oblivion," until through the genius of
"summer's/ Imagination" he becomes fact composed in
a structure of fiction. This is the imagination's "golden
rescue" from the poverty of fact as it is to fact as we want
it to be; the rescue of winter by summer.

Poetry is the finite embodiment of the infinite idea of
the hero, for he exists beyond, always in the end untouch-
able: "There are more heroes than marbles of them./
The marbles are pinchings of an idea,/ Yet there is that

idea behind the marbles." It is Stevens' belief in this idea—
for "The hero is not a person"—that constitutes his faith.
Stevens' statues are emblems of *an* idea of the hero and
incorporate his feeling, since it is this feeling that becomes
the desire to transcend oneself: "It is not an image. It is a
feeling./ There is no image of the hero./ There is a feeling as definition." The quest for the hero is part of the
quest to learn as much about reality as we can. Continually
seeking out the hero while discarding all worn and rusted
images of him, Stevens insists we remember it is not the
hero who was false but our imaginings of him, which continually need revitalization (pp. 280–281):

Each false thing ends. The bouquet of summer
Turns blue and on its empty table
It is stale and the water is discolored.
True autumn stands then in the doorway.
After the hero, the familiar
Man makes the hero artificial.
But was the summer false? The hero?
How did we come to think that autumn
Was the veritable season, that familiar
Man was the veritable man? So

Summer, jangling the savagest diamonds and
Dressed in its azure-doubled crimsons,
May truly bear its heroic fortunes
For the large, the solitary figure.

If we could construct a final image of him, pin him to a
definition, he would cease to be the hero. Our images of
him are never complete and our feelings for him come
closest to forming a definition. Our belief in the hero
directs our energy in the continuous attempt to add to our
lives by seeing reality imaginatively, and Stevens explains
in "Paisant Chronicle" (p. 334) that heroes, the "major
men,"

      . . . are characters beyond
Reality, composed thereof. They are
The fictive man created out of men.
They are men but artificial men. They are
Nothing in which it is not possible
To believe.

"It is the subject in poetry that releases the energy of
the poet" (*Nec. Ang.*, p. 96), and so it is with Stevens'
belief in the hero. In "The Man with the Blue Guitar" (p.

165) the people, believing in the idea of the hero, demand of the poet: " 'But play, you must,/ A tune beyond us, yet ourselves.' " And it is this "tune beyond us" that the people want the poet to make real, they want it to be "A tune upon the blue guitar/ Of things exactly as they are." The people ask the poet to resolve fact as they would like it to be with fact as it is, but the poet replies: "I sing a hero's head, large eye/ And bearded bronze, but not a man." The hero lives only through our imaginations, in our poems, and it is there that we meet and know him. Thus, while thinking of ourselves and what we may come to be, everything about us increases in stature, as it does for "A Pastoral Nun" (p. 378):

Finally, in the last year of her age,
Having attained a present blessedness,
She said poetry and apotheosis are one.

This is the illustration that she used:
If I live according to this law I live
In an immense activity, in which

Everything becomes morning, summer, the hero . . .

Poetry, as the major activity of the imagination, is our guide in the attempt to re-create ourselves in the image of what we feel we ought to be. This image is the myth of the Self as hero, a secular myth appropriate to our time, by which Stevens attempts man's "apotheosis." The hero is an abstraction, but as he appears in each poem he becomes the concretization of the ideal. Since the source of fiction, Stevens argues, is truth, so the source for the myth of the hero lies in man's very nature, and from this origin our fictions and our myths continue to evolve: "There was a myth before the myth began,/ Venerable and articulate and complete./ From this the poem springs" (p. 383).

The origin of myth is grounded in reality but may be revealed by an afflatus of the imagination: "The first idea is an imagined thing" (p. 387). The hero exists not merely because we have invented images of him, but because he prevails when our images of him have been rejected, rising again since there is something within ourselves that demands his presence in spite of our inability to name him conclusively (pp. 387–388):

> . . . But apotheosis is not
> The origin of the major man. He comes,

Compact in invincible foils, from reason,
Lighted at midnight by the studious eye,
Swaddled in revery, the object of

The hum of thoughts evaded in the mind,
Hidden from other thoughts, he that reposes
On a breast forever precious for that touch,

For whom the good of April falls tenderly,
Falls down, the cock-birds calling at the time.
My dame, sing for this person accurate songs.

He is and may be but oh! he is, he is,
This foundling of the infected past, so bright,
So moving in the manner of his hand.

Yet look not at his colored eyes. Give him
No names. Dismiss him from your images.
The hot of him is purest in the heart.

The poet attempts through these limited images and descriptions of the hero to express the final abstraction of
him that embodies the possibilities of man. "The major
abstraction is the idea of man/ And major man is its ex-

ponent." The imagery giving concretization to this abstraction of the hero closely resembles the imagery Stevens uses to describe "nothingness": images of light, transparency, reflectability (as glass or diamond), and the main aspects of the hero, like "nothingness," are his vividness and inclusiveness as possibility.

In "Chocorua to Its Neighbor" (p. 296) Chocorua is a large mountain speaking to its fellow promontory about the idea of man:

To speak quietly at such a distance, to speak
And to be heard is to be large in space,
That, like your own, is large, hence, to be part
Of sky, of sea, large earth, large air. It is
To perceive men without reference to their form.

To perceive men without reference to their form is to know them as an abstraction. Chocorua says that "to speak/ And to be heard is to be large in space," and it is this largeness that likens man to the mountain. In abstraction, then, man also emulates the largeness of sky, sea, earth and air. Chocorua continues, speaking of the coming of this man-as-idea:

159

At the end of night last night a crystal star,
The crystal-pointed star of morning, rose
And lit the snow to a light congenial
To this prodigious shadow, who then came
In an elemental freedom, sharp and cold.

The hero rises on a winter morning, the time when
reality is perceived as fact. The images here, providing
the first description of the hero, are: crystal star, lighted
snow, prodigious shadow; all images of light and reflection. The earliest feelings we have for him will soon fill
us with a sense of illumination and magnitude, for "The
feeling of him was the feel of day,/ And of a day as yet
unseen, in which/ To see was to be." The body's form
cannot contain him ("To think of him destroyed the
body's form"), he needs something larger, and Stevens
attempts to render the idea of his limitlessness even beyond form by telling us "He was a shell of dark blue
glass, or ice,/ Or air collected in a deep essay,/ Or light
embodied." Blue (the symbolic color of the imagination)
predominates in his composition. Again, Stevens uses
light imagery to suggest the transparency through which

the imagination sees into possibility: glass, ice, air, embodied light. And again Stevens gives us a sense of the hero's great size: "He was as tall as a tree in the middle of/ The night. The substance of his body seemed/ Both substance and non-substance, luminous flesh/ Or shapely fire." Along with his qualities of size and light, there is also an awareness of his spiritual immanence. Chocorua continues to develop his ideas about the abstraction of man, as man the hero:

Upon my top he breathed the pointed dark.
He was not man yet he was nothing else.
If in the mind, he vanished, taking there
The mind's own limits, like a tragic thing
Without existence, existing everywhere.

Chocorua himself is dwarfed by the hero's largeness, for as an abstraction of the imagination the hero's existence is limited only by the imagination's ability to conceive of him. Therefore, he is both of man and beyond him at once.

The hero is the central poet whose meditation, theoretically, covers all reality "He breathed in crystal-pointed change the whole/ Experience of night." And yet even this reality turns out to be not all, so that the hero recognizes his finitude in that he knows "that life/ Itself is like a poverty in the space of life." He possesses the wisdom that there is always something more he can be, and he feels the desire for further life because his imagination can conceive the idea of it. He himself is composed of the same desire in us for greater and more abundant life: "He rose because men wanted him to be." He is everything we are and everything that is beyond us, "part desire and part the sense/ Of what men are." Although he is not a human individual, the hero is the essence of human qualities, so that he becomes, for Stevens, the major subject of poetry. And so Stevens, as Chocorua, says, "To speak humanly from the height or from the depth/ Of human things, that is acutest speech./ Now, I, Chocorua, speak of this shadow as/ A human thing." But as our imagination and its speech undergoes its cyclical change—rejecting, restoring and always evolving—our images of the hero change just as our vision of "summer-reality" changes from that of "winter-reality." And yet our original feeling for the hero prevails:

> . . . It is an eminence,
> But of nothing, trash of sleep that will disappear
> With the special things of night, little by little,
> In day's constellation, and yet remain, yet be . . .

The abstraction of the hero emerges from "nothing" just as the "supreme fiction" does, and it also must return to "nothing" to be freshly reimagined. Night and moonlight become day and sunlight just as summer becomes winter. Our vision of the hero when we awake in the morning may appear in retrospect as the "trash of sleep," for the day demands new images and a freshened conception, but our desire for the hero, and our belief that he can evolve from what is real, endures as the energy of our imagination.

The idea of the hero may be taken to heart and may profoundly influence the way in which men live their lives, for where he is, Chocorua says, "the air changes and grows fresh to breathe./ The air changes, creates and re-creates, like strength,/ And to breathe is a fulfilling of desire,/ A clearing, a detecting, a completing,/ A largeness lived and not conceived." Each myth of the hero provides us with a sense of greatness beyond ourselves. Chocorua, great himself, refers to it as "the companion of presences/ Greater than mine, of his demanding, head/ And, of human realizings, rugged roy . . ." As ideal, the hero imposes a demand on those who believe in him, and this demand constitutes an aspect of "human realizings." The very last words of the poem are vague though suggestive. The word "rugged" suggests a crudeness, as if our conception of the hero was still undeveloped. The spirit of the last lines is one of beginning: it is dawn, in earliest winter. "Chocorua to Its Neighbor," terminating with three dots, does not really end, but anticipates the next poem, the newest imagining of the hero.

We turn and return to the hero as we do to reality, and, as Stevens says in "A Primitive Like an Orb" (p. 440), "It is a giant, always, that is evolved." This "giant of nothingness," abstracted from human life by the imagination as an ideal and glorified in our poems, represents the realms of possibility open to man. The concept of "nothingness" expresses Stevens' belief in the infinity of reality; similarly, the hero is the expression of his belief in the infinite possibility of man and his imagination. The

poet, Stevens feels, must live with this belief in the
"giant" and in the "larger poem" in which the greater
hero will be composed, and this can take place, marvel-
ously enough, on "An Ordinary Evening in New Haven"
(p. 465):

As part of the never-ending meditation,
Part of the question that is a giant himself:
Of what is this house composed if not of the sun,

These houses, these difficult objects, dilapidate
Appearances of what appearances,
Words, lines, not meanings, not communications,

Dark things without a double, after all,
Unless a second giant kills the first—
A recent imagining of reality,

Much like a new resemblance of the sun,
Down-pouring, up-springing and inevitable,
A larger poem for a larger audience.

SEVEN

The Feeling of Thought

The house was quiet and the world was calm.
The reader became the book; and summer night
Was like the conscious being of the book.

As a philosophic poet, Stevens' subjects are ideas, concepts and abstractions, not only objects and sensations. But, unlike that of the formal philosopher, his problem is to communicate the experience of having an idea as well as to express the idea itself. To have an idea, Stevens believes, is also to have a feeling—the feeling of that idea, and the logic that brings together one idea with another is itself an emotion, for it is the action of the imagination which always works toward the unification of the abstract and the personal, the rational and the irrational. Theoretically, an idea has a validity independent of any personal conceptualizations of it. This, for Stevens, is idea as fact and not as experience. But experience is dependent upon fact, and it is from this dependency that the imagination flourishes and builds a reality of fact, yet beyond it. The

169

duality of idea and the experience of that idea is exactly like the duality of a material object as fact and apperception of that object. The apperception of an object is an image, or "seeming," so that "every image is the elaboration of a particular of the subject of the image" and also "every image is a restatement of the subject of the image in terms of an attitude" (*Nec. Ang.,* pp. 127, 128). The awareness of these dualities creates a tension in the mind, from which Stevens composes much of his poetry. When he writes about ideas and abstractions he presents them to the reader in a language exuberant with his own feeling; he gives us at once both thought and the experience of thinking. And, in addition, the experience of thinking itself becomes a subject for Stevens' poems, so that both in practice and in theory Stevens demonstrates and explores the drama of the mind.

The theme of "Metaphors of a Magnifico" (p. 19) can be most accurately expressed as a question: How does the mind act when it is trying to concentrate on an abstract idea? The idea in this poem is the relationship of the *one* to the *many,* and a magnifico, a grand man of high position, is trying to puzzle this idea through. He says:

Twenty men crossing a bridge,
Into a village,
Are twenty men crossing twenty bridges,
Into twenty villages,
Or one man
Crossing a single bridge into a village.

But this proposition does not satisfy the magnifico, it does
not seem to have any application, as if its meaning existed
in limbo, so that the magnifico thinks: "This is old song/
That will not declare itself." And with this rejection, he
then tries to simplify his idea from a statement about a
theoretical relationship to a statement as recognition of
fact:

Twenty men crossing a bridge,
Into a village,
Are
Twenty men crossing a bridge
Into a village.

But this proposition too, though "certain as meaning,"
seems pointless to the magnifico and, therefore, like the

first proposition, it "will not declare itself." This idea, however, having moved the magnifico's mind closer to the fact of the men and the bridge from a theoretical abstraction, serves as a transition from conception to perception. The magnifico has ceased in his speculation, and what now hold his thought are the vivid, particular images and sounds that greet his eyes and ears:

The boots of the men clump
On the boards of the bridge.
The first white wall of the village
Rises through fruit-trees.

Such perception is so specific, so certain, that even the memory of the subject of his abstract speculation dims, and the magnifico remarks: "Of what was it I was thinking?/ So the meaning escapes." And the only thing that remains fixed in his mind is the observation, "The first white wall of the village . . ./ The fruit trees. . . ." The point of the poem is that the mind must always turn to perception for the foundation of its thought, and Stevens' success is that he dramatizes this truth, reveals the workings of the mind, without having to generalize about it.

What is there in the ordinary, in the daily comedy of our lives, that is unusual, special, intense, except the elaborations of thought rising from the observation of common things? Is to see something only to see it, to have a steady image on the screen of the mind? Or, are not the simplest objects "fluttering things" that our images belie when we fix them in our descriptions in a single pose? Though our thought must return to immediate perceptual observation after its abstract flight, as Stevens shows in "Metaphors of a Magnifico," is sight so simple that to see is to know, that what we see exists exactly as we see it? If this were true, all knowledge would be purely intellectual, without symbols, allusions or indirections, but only the perfect image of the thing itself, representing itself. All feeling and irrationality would be absent, for nothing of ourselves would be part of the things we see. We *will* to see things as they are, but the impossibility of success rescues the irrational and all our feeling. The paradox explaining this impossibility is that, though we see specific qualities and though these qualities seem absolute, we discover that there is no end to the specific things we can see, no end then to our factlike descriptions of what we see, and therefore no limited number of specific details or the data of sight can define the reality of any object. And herein lies the power of experience, for it brings us into relationship with whatever we see and our descriptions then are choices, but choices made only for an instant, for we live in a dynamic dialectic with the world.

In "Study of Two Pears" (p. 196) Stevens, in setting out to paint a still-life picture of the pears, begins with the assumption that the pears can be absolutely defined, drawn to the fact of what they are. It is a scholarly or a scientific assumption, and so Stevens starts appropriately by saying, "Opusculum paedagogum," and finishes the first stanza by telling us what the pears are not, delineating, so to speak, the field of consideration: "The pears are not viols,/ Nudes or bottles./ They resemble nothing else." The image of the pears is to be seen in isolation, as a reproduction only of their properties and qualities, without any similes, resemblances or correspondences. The details Stevens gives us of the pears are acute and vivid: "They are yellow forms/ Composed of curves/ Bulging toward the base." "A hard dry leaf hangs/ From the stem.." Our eye responds to the richness and nuances of their coloring: "They are touched red." "In the way they are modelled/ There are bits of blue." "The yellow glistens./ It glistens with various yellows,/ Citrons, oranges and greens,/ Flowering over the skin." And just as we would believe that we know these pears, know them as they are in the final strict image of them, Stevens subtly leads our observation beyond them to their shadows and then to the tablecloth: "The shadows of the pears/ Are blobs on the green cloth." No longer do the pears exist by themselves and no longer can the observer hold them in isolation or fix them in a description: "The pears are not seen/ As the observer wills." At this realization, the observer himself has come into full existence. He is not merely the consciousness passively reflecting the image of the pears, but is an independent power, a will, that cannot ultimately know, yet always can experience.

Experience is always transcendent, for it is more than the sum of its parts. It always contains the tension of what is and what might be; it brings together the rational and the irrational, the actual and the imaginary. It is an event abstracted, and an abstraction embodied. And so presence, the living moment, is infinite beyond all our descriptions of that moment, beyond our histories that record it. And so Stevens tells us in "Bouquet of Belle Scavoir" (p. 231) that no symbol, image or memory of a woman that a man loves can substitute for her company, the mystery of her presence, for "It is she alone that matters." The rose in her bouquet symbolizes her to her lover, who knows that "It is easy to say/ The figures of speech, as why she chose/ This dark, particular rose./ Everything in it is herself." And yet he also knows that this flower is not only a symbol, but a thing in itself, a thing that demands its own attention and must be seen for its own qualities: "Yet the freshness of the leaves, the burn/ Of the colors, are tinsel changes,/ Out of the changes of both light and dew." Thus to see the rose as symbol is also to see the rose as rose and to be reminded that it is the symbol, not the lover, that is present. Each reminiscence of her only emphasizes the fact that she is not there and each thought of her intensifies the pang in the realization of her absence:

The thought of her takes her away.
The form of her in something else
Is not enough.
The reflection of her here, and then there,
Is another shadow, another evasion,
Another denial. If she is everywhere,
She is nowhere, to him.

In this way Stevens argues that experience is indivisible. It is neither fact nor impression, but both. All material existence has its extension in the imagination, and only then does it truly exist. There is no beloved without a lover, and from their union each takes his own reality, a reality of presence, of being, so that Stevens says, "It is she that he wants, to look at directly,/ Someone before him to see and to know."

"To know," in Stevens' meaning, is never anything less than the consciousness of emotional, irrational forces working together with the very consciousness that is aware of them. A feeling is not completely felt until one is aware that one has the feeling, until part of the feeling is a thought. So thought and feeling are not separate, but interdependent, and the irrationality of feeling is a fact of "human presence" that thought must always consider, and to which it is tied. And though we live freely, guided by our intelligence, nevertheless, the mind flourishes only from the soil of experience, from the initial presence of being. This relationship Stevens dramatizes in the dialogue of "Saint John and the Back-Ache" (p. 436):

The Back-Ache
   The mind is the terriblest force in the world, father,
   Because, in chief, it, only, can defend
   Against itself. At its mercy, we depend
   Upon it.
Saint John
         The world is presence and not force.
   Presence is not mind.

                    . . . . .
   It fills the being before the mind can think.

                    . . . . .
The Back-Ache
   Presence lies far too deep, for me to know
   Its irrational reaction, as from pain.

As son depends upon father for existence, and father on son for continuity, so do reality and imagination depend upon each other, so do feeling and thought, pleasure and pain. Form distinguishes existence from chaos because it is based on relationships. "To know" is to recognize the world as a structure of relationships, of resemblances and correspondences, and to feel that one belongs to this structure. And "to love," in Stevens' meaning, is to feel the intensity of this belonging in that it relates, each in his unique way, man to man, man to woman, and man to his work and his world, and to feel that this belonging is sufficient—the source of final peace and acceptance.

Stevens' last song of peace and acceptance is sung as the "Final Soliloquy of the Interior Paramour" (p. 524). The "paramour" is the lover of the world and is "interior" because it is the imagination that conceives of such an encompassing love that gives everything an order to which we belong, belonging with others. In this idea, in the imaginative order, feeling and thought become one in a unity of experience—the experience of love:

Light the first light of evening, as in a room
In which we rest and, for small reason, think
The world imagined is the ultimate good.

179

This is, therefore, the intensest rendezvous.
It is in that thought that we collect ourselves,
Out of all the indifferences, into one thing:

Within a single thing, a single shawl
Wrapped tightly round us, since we are poor, a warmth,
A light, a power, the miraculous influence.

Here, now, we forget each other and ourselves.
We feel the obscurity of an order, a whole,
A knowledge, that which arranged the rendezvous.

Within its vital boundary, in the mind.
We say God and the imagination are one . . .
How high that highest candle lights the dark.

Out of this same light, out of the central mind,
We make a dwelling in the evening air,
In which being there together is enough.

EIGHT

Style: the Pleasures
of Personality

Poetry
Exceeding music must take the place
Of empty heaven and its hymns,
Ourselves in poetry must take their place.

One of the first things to catch the attention in reading Wallace Stevens' poetry is the unusual variety of his vocabulary. No other poet can equal it. Included in this marvel of words are the unfamiliar and unusual, archaic usages, foreign words, names of places, flowers, plants, birds, invented sounds and words. Just a short sampling will illustrate the point: paladins, oblation, fubbed, girandoles, fabliau, canna, gobbet, princox, funest, Tallapoosa, rattapallax, Tehuantepec, gelosa, gaudium, hidalgo, spissantly, nougats, fusky, ephebe, effendi, millefiori, curule, accelerando, gilderlinged. These words are not used as substitutes for more familiar words, but each in its context is precisely meant so that no other word could replace it. Yet, for Stevens, the unit of speech is not the word, but the phrase or line. Words are used to add to the acceleration of the rhythmical flow rather than to exercise their inertia as a single beat.

Stevens' rhetoric is euphuistic only for ironic purposes, when it is his artistic intent to call attention to the self-consciousness of language or to make a point about the necessary self-consciousness of the poet. In any other case, what may appear to be contrived becomes quite natural as a familiarity with the poem is reached. The eloquence of Stevens' speech is all contained, controlled, graceful and relaxing. In addition to the inexorable movement of his lines, the felicity of his rhythms, there are other elements contributing to the total effect of grand rhetoric. The sense of musical expectation and presence is always high, although we are never certain of how this expectation will be fulfilled. The meter follows or subtly departs from a basic line of iambic pentameter. The poems in *Harmonium* adhere most closely to this meter, but Stevens' line moves with some irregularity in some later poems—such as "Notes toward a Supreme Fiction." He never rhymes regularly, but uses to great effect the occasional or unexpected rhyme. In *Harmonium* there is more rhyming than in the later volumes, but this is only speaking of end-rhymes, for Stevens continues to use internal rhymes and off-rhymes [Italics mine—R.P.]:

Then from their poverty they rose,
From dry *guitars*, and to *catarrhs*
They flitted
Through the palace walls.

Sister and mother and diviner love,
And of the sisterhood of the living *dead*
Most *near*, most *clear*, and of the *clear*est bloom,
And of the fragrant mothers the most *dear*
And queen, and of diviner love the day
And flames and summer and sweet fire, no *thread*
Of cloudy silver sprinkles in your *gown*
Its venon of *renown*, and on your *head*
No *crown* is simpler than the simple hair.

And *reaches, beaches,* tomorrow's *regions* became
One thinking of apocalyptic *legions.*

He enjoys putting sound clusters together, as in "Bantams in Pine-Woods" (p. 75):

185

Chieftain Iffucan of Azcan in caftan
Of tan with henna hackles, halt!

and in "On the Road Home" (p. 103):

It was at that time, that the silence was larg*est*
And long*est,* the night was round*est,*
The fragrance of the autumn warm*est,*
Clos*est* and strong*est.*

He will use, either terminally or internally, assonances
and consonances. Occasionally, he will use other rhetorical
devices, but the music of related sound that he employs
most often is that of alliteration:

Large-*m*annered *m*otions to his *m*ythy *m*ind
He *m*oved a*m*ong us, as a *m*uttering king,
*M*agnificant, would *m*ove a*m*ong his hinds.

The pines along the river and the dry men *b*lown
*B*rown as the *b*read, thinking of *b*irds
Flying from *b*urning countries and *b*rown sand shores.

186

Wrapped in their seemings, *c*rowd on *c*urious *c*rowd.

In perpetual *r*evolution, *r*ound and *r*ound.

Like *r*ubies *r*eddened by *r*ubies *r*eddening.

*D*ang*l*ing and *sp*ang*l*ing, like the *m*ic-*m*ac of *m*ocking birds.

Stevens' description in praise of the musical character of T. S. Eliot's "Rhapsody on a Windy Night," as much describes his own poetry as it does Eliot's: "This is a specimen of what is meant by music today. It contains rhymes at irregular intervals and it is intensely cadenced" (*Nec. Ang.,* p. 125). One might call this statement Stevens' credo for composition if we add to it his whimsy for musical effects: sound clusters, alliteration, invented sounds ("thunder's rattapallax"), sounds of instruments ("squiggling like saxophones" or "bubbling of bassoons"). He says: "If occasionally the poet touches the triangle or one of the cymbals, he does it only because he feels like doing it" (*Nec. Ang.,* p. 126).

Stevens tells us that "the poet manifests his personality, first of all, by his choice of subject" (*Nec. Ang.,* p. 20), which for him is the quotidian, the ordinary and the imagination, or, as he says in "Of Modern Poetry" (p. 239), "The poem of the mind in the act of finding/ What will suffice." He then goes on to say that "The second way by which a poet manifests his personality is by his style" (*Nec. Ang.*, p. 123). The sensuous richness that characterizes Stevens' poetry is achieved through an opulence of color, sound, image and noun. We are always given a scene, a specific sense of being in the world. Besides inventing words like "rattapallax," Stevens will vary an existing word to suit his own poetical needs and his taste for particular sounds. See how the word "nincompated" becomes the perfect adjective for "pedagogue" in its context in "Comedian as the Letter C" (p. 27). "Nincompated," of course, is Stevens' invention from nincompoop. He will also use archaic forms if he likes their sound, such as "shapen snow." In another such instance he speaks of an "isle/ Melodious, where spirits *gat* them home." Not only the word order but also the subject of this passage is in perfect harmony with the archaic "gat." For Stevens a word is part of a feeling. "Words add to the senses," we are told. And certain phrases are particularly characteristic, such as "were one" or "are one." This is important, because it is an often-repeated example of Stevens' abiding concern with the reconciliation of conflicting or contradictory forces: "The false and the true are one," or "But we and the diamond globe at last were one."

Stevens' verbal wit and ironic tone are central to his style. But it is never a vicious wit or a tragic irony, for he does not attempt to evoke our pity or compassion. It is a comic irony that enables Stevens to see the many possible sides of an issue and, in a sense, to take them all. It is an irony that brings together both consciousness and self-consciousness, and in accomplishing this the Self always sees its own limitations and comic finitude. A technique by which Stevens often achieves this particular ironic effect may perhaps be accurately described as the use of "inner wit," as, for example, in "Connoisseur of Chaos" (p. 215), in which Stevens speaks directly to his reader, saying:

After all the pretty contrast of life and death
Proves that these opposite things partake of one,
At least that was the theory, when bishops' books

Resolved the world. We cannot go back to that.
The squirming facts exceed the squamous mind,
If one may say so. [Italics mine—R.P.]

The "If one may say so" calls further attention to the exaggerated claims and language of the preceding lines and lends a humor and perspective to Stevens' ideas. Sometimes a humorous or ironic effect is achieved by the juxtaposition of the silly and the serious or the colloquial and the rhetorical: "Hi! The creator too is blind," and, "Ludwig Richter, turbulent Schlemihl,/ Has lost the whole in which he was contained."

More than anywhere else, Stevens' irony and humor is to be found in his titles: the silly and serious adjacent, the play on words, the tongue-in-cheek statement, and the sarcastic. For example: "A High-Toned old Christian Woman," "The Emperor of Ice-Cream," "The Revolutionists Stop for Orangeade," "Anatomy of Monotony," "United Dames of America," "Anything Is Beautiful if You Say It Is," "Extracts from Addresses to the Academy of Fine Ideas," "Sad Strains of a Gay Waltz," "The Pleasures of Merely Circulating," "Holiday in Reality," "Continual Conversation with a Silent Man," "The Prejudice against the Past," "The Owl in the Sarcophagus," "Saint John and the Back-Ache." Stevens' titles are like the characters in a drama. Each poem must be regarded from the point of view of its speaker or from what mood it is being spoken, just as we interpret the speeches by a character in a play from what we know of that character. Stevens has many moods in which he is not strictly speaking in his own voice or seeing things through his own eyes, and his titles give us the necessary perspective for reading these poems.

Stevens' verse is mostly expository. When he has several ideas with which he wants to deal, he will consider them one against the other, trying to see what can be resolved. He may look at one object, or take a single idea, and examine the many ways in which it may be regarded, and to do this he often uses a "theme and variations" form as in "Earthy Anecdote" (p. 3):

Every time the bucks went clattering
Over Oklahoma
A firecat bristled in the way.

191

Wherever they went,
They went clattering,
Until they swerved
In a swift, circular line
To the right,
Because of the firecat.

Or until they swerved
In a swift, circular line
To the left,
Because of the firecat.

The bucks clattered.
The firecat went leaping,
To the right, to the left,
And
Bristled in the way.

Later, the firecat closed his bright eyes
And slept.

The firecat, satiated with his meal of a buck, completes a
form in nature just as the structure of the poem completes
an art-form. Both are part of the earthy anecdote.

Some poems are more obvious as theme and variation compositions, such as "Thirteen Ways of Looking at a Blackbird" (p. 92) or "Variations on a Summer Day" (p. 232). But particularly when he is describing something he has carefully observed, Stevens adheres to a strict theme and variations form. His knowledge of music is his source for this form, and "The Man with the Blue Guitar" (thirty-three variations) is his major achievement with this technique. His poetry is filled with references to musical instruments and with imitations of musical sounds and the songs of birds. And all this musical effect has its philosophical counterpart, for it represents Stevens' search for "that right sound, that song/ . . . that remains and sings/ In the high imagination, triumphantly."

A fundamental distinction between symbolism and allegory is, perhaps, that the relationship between the symbol and whatever it symbolizes is a natural one, while in allegory the relationship of a sign and what it signifies is arbitrary. The symbol spontaneously evokes a response in us, while an allegorical sign is chosen intellectually. A symbol is connotative because it is directed toward our cognitive faculty. The former *represents,* as for example,

Melville's whale suggests the forbidding mystery of infinite power; and the latter *means,* in the way a green traffic light means "go."

Stevens uses no symbols like Yeats' tower or gyre, or Eliot's desert or rose garden, but when he is talking about "reality" the associated images he consistently gives us are: earth, rock, sun, day, green, north, winter, nature and body; when he is talking about the "imaginary," the associated images are: musical instruments, air, moon, night, blue, south, summer, art and mind. The feeling one has reading Stevens is that these images work both allegorically and symbolically; there is something arbitrary about them, and yet something natural too. For example, blue does seem to be a more internal color than green, it seems to recede, to move inward, and so it is well chosen as the imagination's color.

The merging of the abstract and the mental with the concrete and the sensual is perhaps the most characteristic quality of Stevens' style. If a poem begins with a generalization, he will proceed to illustrate it, or, if a poem commences with a series of illustrative particulars, it will end with a generalization. Stevens asks, "Is the poem both peculiar and general?" and his poetry provides an affirmative answer. In "Anecdote of Men by the Thousand" (p. 51) he begins with a general statement: "The soul, he said, is composed/ Of the external world," and the rest of the poem consists of a series of examples proving this thesis:

The dress of a woman of Lhassa,
In its place,
Is an invisible element of that place
Made visible.

In "Man Carrying Thing" (p. 350) the same technique is used:

The poem must resist the intelligence
Almost successfully. Illustration:

A brune figure in winter resists
Identity.

The poem continues with additional illustrations until the point is fully made. In "What We See Is What We

Think" (p. 459) he begins with a generalization in the title and then traces a series of particular observations and ideas which alter this thesis until he reaches its opposite, which is then stated as a generalization in the poem's last line: "Since what we think is never what we see." The illustrative and the theoretical are always contending in the development of a Stevens poem. Theory derived from observation and logic, and fact clarified by theory, is Stevens' double concern. He is fascinated equally by the most rarefied abstraction and the most subtle nuance or detail of appearance.

Stevens' poems always set a scene but rarely present a situation, and the reader seldom has the sense that a poem is addressed to a particular person or written about a special character. The love poems are not passionate or intimate, since, for the most part, they are written to the world, and to the reader. The moments of greatest intensity are those of philosophical acceptance and sensuous or aesthetic appreciation, and there are no moments of rage, despair, humiliation, grief, desperation or hatred. The drama at which his style aims is contained in this challenge and proposition: how can the imagination transform and create a world that would satisfy its own desire for a paradise? And the lyric feeling his style seeks is the spontaneous pleasure of sensation and a new ordering of reality.

To speak of Stevens as possessing a "comic spirit" is to place him not in a tradition but in a genre. It is primarily a descriptive phrase by which to indicate Stevens' concern with speech and thought rather than with character and action, and to suggest that there is a lightness, a wit, an irony and a humor to Stevens' tone and style rather than somberness, bitterness or any weight of personal suffering. Tragedy fixes its vision on the terrible things and events that lead man to wisdom and reveal—though perhaps at the very moment of loss or death—that life is strong and good. The comic vision inherits, rather than earns, this affirmation or optimism; it belong to the world of Ferdinand and Miranda after the trials and success of Prospero. It is not less honest or less true than tragedy, but it is predicated on a different experience. It is aware of pain and evil, and even anticipates them, but it is not in the process of suffering because of them. The luxury of this comfort and this well-being is that it allows men to explore the range of their thoughts, to experience the variety of sensuous pleasures, and with this luxury Stevens achieves his success and conceives of an earthly paradise in some of the most witty, profound and beautiful poems in the English language.

Index of the Works of Wallace Stevens
Cited and Quoted

All quotations from the works of Wallace Stevens come from *The Necessary Angel, The Collected Poems of Wallace Stevens* and *Opus Posthumous,* published by Alfred A. Knopf, Incorporated.